M000217754

PSYCHED ON SERVICE

DAVID M. CORBIN

SIGMA BUSINESS PUBLISHING

New York, NY   2002

i

PSYCHED ON SERVICE

Copyright © 2002 by David Corbin

Third printing

All rights reserved. No part of this book may be reproduced or utilized in any form or by any means, electronic or mechanical, including photocopying, recording or by any information storage and retrieval systems, without permission in writing from the author.

Publisher's Cataloging in Publication Data

(Prepared by Sigma Business Publishing)

Corbin, David M.

Psyched On Service

ISBN0-9715455-0-2

1. PSYCHED ON SERVICE

Contributing Editor .... John Carroll
Cover Design .... Carolyn Mickelson
Original Illustrations .... Elain Ng

Printed in the United States of America.

PSYCHED ON SERVICE

"Psyched On Service is loaded with brilliant, instantly useable ideas on how to deliver extraordinary customer service to everyone, every time." - Mark Victor Hanson
Co-creator, #1 New York Times best selling series **Chicken Soup for the Soul**®
Co-Author, **The One Minute Millionaire**

"Psyched On Service offers practical strategies for businesses small or large, new or established, growing or cutting back. Any business that relies on customers to grow and thrive will benefit from the ideas in this book." – Tony Alessandra, PhD, CSP, CPAE
Author, **The Platinum Rule**
Author, **Charisma**

"Service to be efficient, needs good systems. Service, to be valuable and impactful, needs integrity and caring. Dave Corbin brings the Synapse between these through his models and stories in Psyched On Service. An inspiring and easy read, which offers lasting insights on service." - Jim Cathcart
Author, **Relationship Selling**

"Your ability to deliver excellent customer service will determine your success or failure. This book shows you how!" – Brian Tracy
Author, **Maximum Achievement: Strategies and Skills That Will Unlock Your Hidden Powers to Succeed**

DEDICATION

Sometimes I feel like I'm the real life Forrest Gump, not necessarily the brightest bulb on the shelf but certainly the luckiest. Luckily, my family, friends, colleagues and, yes, clients have offered up their enlightenment to me from time to time. I happily acknowledge them below and in the Gratitude section of this book.

Special thanks to my wonderful family, Adriane, Jenna, Ben, Ellie, Henry, Edith, Howie, Carol, and the whole clan-Iris, Karl, Lori, Eric, Adam, Michelle, Lainie, Richard, Rob, Nikki, Paul, Eva Brooke, – and I'm blessed with a large and wonderful family, too many to mention.

Through the years I have had many business partners. One business partner who has been there for me through it all is my wife Adriane. Your counsel is of greater value that you'll ever know. I thank you and love you very much.

TABLE OF CONTENTS

CHAPTER 3

CHAPTER 4

CHAPTER 5

INTRODUCTION

Too many companies have invested too much money in training and development with the only result being a smaller bank account and a cynical workforce. It's as though they thought throwing money at the challenge was going to make it "all better" or better yet, "just go away". I've seen that, haven't you?

The *Unfailing Step-By-Step Guide to Professional Success and Personal Perfection* is not currently available in stores. And it never will be. If you find a copy, throw it away. It's trash and you don't need it.

Why do we need another person's dogmatic opinions on how to manage a business, on how to manage ourselves and read others? Well, we don't... and this book doesn't profess to do so.

This book is the best tool for any business professional to create a positive service culture because it includes solid tactics, strategies and, perhaps most importantly, sensitivities that we've experienced and witnessed in service excellent companies which means to you, dear reader, increased peace of mind, productivity and many of the other seductive goals of life and business. The reason I write this is because you probably want to know what is store for you, right?

It bears pointing out that this book does not

intend to prescribe a ready remedy for the challenges of any particular business. The Psyched On Service Mentality is not a rigid platform of ideas, but a flexible program for understanding your business from a different view, a marketing point of view among others. It gives you the tools to understand and diagnose the difficulties that come about in the regular course of business.

I am not a business guru. Sorry. I am a pragmatic entrepreneur who has bootstrapped most of what I've done in business. Many hours perusing books, listening to tapes and attending workshops contributed to my belief that the answers are out there; seek and ye shall find. Hence, much of what I offer here on creating and maintaining a productive service culture is an amalgam of practical possibilities that we've garnered, tried, leveraged, refined and overall "redeemed" in the world of commerce. For example, I can recall vividly attending a full day seminar, which was a total dud... except for one brief five-minute reprise. The speaker offered a simple idea that spawned a world of ideas in my mind, which in turn snowballed and evolved into a method of staff development that has assisted in generating literally millions of dollars thru my career. On top of that, it has helped me to contribute to the development of employees into managers who have added to my businesses and then gone out and created their own successful businesses. I refer to these ideas as practical possibilities because if they are not used, actually put to work, then they simply remain as a possibility. Using them is up to you and I sincerely hope that you do leverage them to great heights of success.

Throughout this book we will utilize an analogy to make some points, an analogy from the field of neurology and physiology; the brain. We all have one. Our success and failures often stem from how well we manage these systems, feed, nurture and utilize our brain.

Synapse: The area of contact from one neuron to another, across which nerve impulses **travel.** The word" synapse" comes from Greek: "syn" meaning "together" and "haptein" meaning "to clasp."

In this book, we refer to the void space as the Disconnect.

Disconnect: the gap between actions, thoughts, processes in which necessary information and/or actions do not connect for fulfillment or to fruition. A great example that many of us relate to is the one where we find ourselves in a room wondering what did I come in here for? Clearly there is a Disconnect between the thought process of going into the room and the continued thought

process as to why we are there. A simple (and pretty common) example, no?

A **disconnect** is a break between these things. It is the place where good intentions fall through the cracks and are never fulfilled. One might find so many New Year's resolutions there, un-mailed letters, intended actions, unexpressed compliments and sympathies, unachieved goals and then like. These things never made it across the great divide and they fell into the depths of darkness.

It's no great shake if the disconnect occurs between your intent to get milk at the store and your remembering to do so. That happens without much damage or remorse. A simple disconnect, no problem.
However, when that disconnect is between your intent to take your insulin and your remembering to do so, then the ramifications can be enormous.

A **synapse** is a bridge or link from one place to another. In this case it is a link
between forgetting and remembering;
between knowing and doing;
between not realizing and realizing;
between unconscious and conscious; and often between failure and success.

Our business, as our lives, can be looked at as a series of these disconnects and synapses.

This book will review some of these gaps and connectors as it relates to personal and professional success. They will be explored and discussed and where applicable, illustrated with specific case examples that we have encountered in the field.

How does an organization get the most out of its personnel? How does the individual professional get the most out of his job? How does one build a winning team of involved, informed, and innovative professionals?

One of the primary tenets of this book is that unless the individual is enrolled into their own personal process of personal and professional development, to the legitimate core concepts associated with these buzzwords, then there is not much of a chance that substantial change will occur.

> **Core Premise:** You and everyone who you work with and know is in business whether they know it or not. We are all in business for ourselves – as we sell our skills, talents, knowledge or whatever deliverables to others. Many of us appear to be employees of yet another company as we sell our time and talent to them in exchange for a check and sometimes more. Make no mistake about it, though, we are really working for ME, Incorporated, so to speak, and at the time that our customer (going by the name of employer) is dissatisfied with ME Inc.'s deliverables they will find a vendor other

than ME Inc. as there are many, many out there trying to get the business.

So, If you are the President of Me, Inc. then it is your responsibility to make certain that your companies output, it's goods and services, is top notch, best of breed. Therefore you are also responsible to oversee that every employee in ME, Inc. (that's you) is totally and completely trained and prepared to deliver an excellent "Psyched on Service" level of professionalism. Hence, make certain that 100% of your employees (that's you, again) is conversant in the principles and strategies in this book.

A former partner of mine, a deservedly famous speaker and author, was once asked why he shared his secrets of success so openly in the presence of his competitors. He noted that their tendency to scurry and write down these words of wisdom was second only to their inability to take solid action on them. Voila! He was right and I often wondered why. Why, if the answer were clearly before them, if their competitive edge was within arms length, would they not take immediate action toward their goals? It made no sense. It makes no sense. Yet it is true. Why? It plagued my thinking. Why don't we lose weight, quit bad habits and generally move in the direction of what we want? We do want them, no?

That is what I have been working on for the
last twenty plus years as a sub-script to my
consulting, speaking, inventing, building of
businesses. Why, I would wonder, would
companies sponsor employees to attend
trainings, lectures, workshops and
symposia, have them attend only to have
them go back to old ways, ways that
preceded their attendance?

INCLUDED IN WHAT FOLLOWS IS A
METHODOLOGY THAT IS THE BEST
WE'VE FOUND TO ENROLL THE
INDIVIDUAL INTO THE PROCESS and
then offer some proven strategies for their use
and benefit. It has worked for us and our client
companies and we have confidence that it will
work for you.

The Psyched On Service Mentality lays the
groundwork for answering all these questions
and many more. It makes the powerful
assertion that the most valuable asset (and one
of the precious few appreciating assets) of any
organization is human. To the individual
professional, this book makes the case that
through personal development and a
rededication to the *organization's* success
come the rewards of professional fulfillment
and increased job security. Among its other
uses, this book teaches how to enlist the
working professional in your vision of
success.

And it works because it comes battle tested and represents the conclusions of over 25 years of consulting experience with organizations as diverse as Bank of America, Motorola, Kaiser Permanente, and the Veterans Administration. The hard-won wisdom, or at least observations, of those 25 years boils down to several easy-to-learn principles. Every business manager knows these principles, maybe as gut intuition, maybe as memories of past mistakes, but she knows them. 25 years of observing the best and worst companies in dozens of industries has left one unmistakable impression: there are reasons some companies are more successful than others. Working with executives and managers at AT&T, Hallmark, Chaparral Steel and others, it became clear that the most productive, the most positive, the most efficient and effective companies all shared five common qualities that led them to succeed.

One of Life's Great Contradictions: Whoever said that gaining wisdom is <u>easy</u> would probably lie about something else too!

We are first taught, "Everything comes to those who wait".

Then we are taught, "The Lord helps those who help themselves."

While not necessarily in that order, these are the messages of wisdom that we are

taught early in life. WELL, WHICH IS IT? IT'S GOT TO BE ONE OR THE OTHER AND THEY'RE CONFUSING THE $%&# OUT OF US! Well, Grasshopper, perhaps we will find the balance... together.

Read on and maybe this will be one of the "truths" revealed in this book. Or maybe not.

It's harder and harder in today's fast changing world for my Mom down in Florida to tell her friends what her youngest son David does to earn a living. The best descriptor for my business advisory services is that of a consultant. However, part of my responsibilities would best describe me less as a consultant and more as an insultant. Sometimes I must, in all good conscience, and with love in my heart, tell the honest truth. Someone's got to tell the emperor that he aint wearin' no clothes.

My esteemed friend and author, Rabbi Sheldon Moss, remarks that most of the year he is tasked with "comforting the *afflicted". However, at other times of the year he reminds us to contribute to the needy, he then needs to "afflict the comfortable". Those who are comfortable need to be afflicted with the realization that others are not so fortunate... an awareness that is usually associated with such sobering events as the World Trade Center attack, etc.*

Some of my clients are comfortable in the way that they conduct their business, ways that may not be serving them positively in the way that they used to. How in good faith, as a consultant, a trusted advisor, can I not mention this observation... and still feel good about what I do? So, that's when the "insultant" appears. So far, so good... no one's taken a swing at me for it, either physically or politically. It's a matter of doing the right thing, taking a stand, and representing the "voice of the business" in an honest, open and caring way. The Consultant must at times be the Insultant. So, if I seem a bit opinionated in this book... it is simply because I AM.

I'm hoping that you'll do more than read this book. The Psyched On Service Mentality is about action. We've seen that when you engage your employees in the Psyched On Service Mentality, when you facilitate their working towards their own success and job security, when you implement a positive work culture that values everyone's opinion, you're going to see results. We're confident of that because we've been there and done that. As this book will show, the employee that feels involved, that feels part of the team, will stay involved and will be far happier and more productive.

Read, re-read and most importantly use the exercises to actually take action, try them on for size, and cash them in. They don't work if you don't. We hope that you use the process that you spread it around your sphere of influence of friends and associates and that you benefit from it as we and our clients have. The Psyched On Service Mentality is about actualizing your company's potential as well as your own. Get excited about doing business, get psyched! The Psyched On Service Mentality begins with the business manager, leader, rapport leader yet its principles work for everybody. Get everyone involved! Let's get started!

All the best,

David Corbin
The Performance Technology Group
San Diego, California

P.S. I invite you to share any questions, examples of "Psyched" applications or comments to Psyched@DavidCorbin.Com

About The Book's Cover

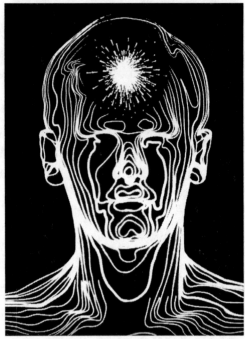

The design of the cover of this book is no accident. Time after time, we found that a critical difference between clients who merely enjoy and appreciate the following information and those who leverage and increase their desired results with it is as follows:

They keep these concepts within mental reach. That is, they keep them in the "front of their mind" and easily accessible to their immediate memory. Hence they have immediate access to the ideas, they use them easily and effortlessly and they derive great benefits. Please allow this icon to serve as a memory jolt to you to keep these ideas in the front of YOUR mind.

Chapter 1
Getting Started

Psyched On Service Mentality? Actualizing my *potential*? *Synapses*? What is this, some new kind of Neo Neurological Yoga for business managers? Time to get naked and jump into a hot tub?

No, this book is about business, building people to achieve business results and nothing else. The five Synapses from which this book takes its title represent five principles without which no business can hope to thrive. This book, rooted in the Psyched On Service Mentality, is an elaboration on these principles.

One of the primary tenets of this book is that unless the individual is enrolled into their own personal process of personal and professional development, to the legitimate core concepts associated with these buzzwords, then there is not much of a chance that substantial change will occur.

So what *are* these five Synapses? They are:

1) **Synapse One:** From brain to action to uphold the credibility and reputation of the company;

2) **Synapse Two:** From brain to action to make the most of all available marketing opportunities;

3) **Synapse Three:** From brain to action to provide the customer with a positive emotional experience;
4) **Synapse Four:** From brain to action to apply the art of damage control;
5) **Synapse Five:** From brain to action to apply the science of interpersonal communication.

These are the Synapses to legendary service, to successful business, to actualized business folk and possibly to a summer home in Tahiti. Furthermore, they are the concrete embodiment of the *Psyched On Service Mentality*. While these Synapses are themselves a practical program for success in business, they are also an example of the Psyched On Service Mentality in action

While the Psyched On Service Mentality can show you the five Synapses to success in business, it's important to remember there are also five really good ways to get wet. For every right way of doing something, there's a way to do it wrong.

What we can do is examine some of the common mistakes that plague businesses in all sectors of the economy. For the individual business manager, it should be as fruitful to examine these mistakes, as it is to review the common strengths of successful businesses.

You can't do it right until you stop doing it wrong. 25 years of conducting and consulting in business has led me to a short list of the five mistakes common to businesses in every industry. The remainder of this book will be devoted largely to identifying the Disconnects, troubleshooting these mistakes and building the Synapses to connect the needs with the solutions.

They are:

1) **Disconnect One:** Gap between employee's *knowledge* and *action* to perform their role in the business' marketing plan.

2) **Disconnect Two:** Gap between opportunity and performance in most internal marketing with customers.

3) **Disconnect Three:** Gap between perceived and true value of its product or service relative to its marketing plan.

4) **Disconnect Four:** The business has no strategy to recover from mistakes, mishaps, and errors. Big Disconnect.

5) **Disconnect Five:** Front-line employees are not taught the communication skills they need to be effective. Skills needed Disconnected from skills available.

Throughout the rest of this book, I will detail these five internal marketing mistakes and propose five solutions; the so-called Disconnects and Synapses to legendary service. These five examples, along with in the field experiences and applications will demonstrate the power of the Psyched On

Service Mentality. The following chapters will show that in sharpening a business' focus on marketing principles and in building team participation among employees, that any organization necessarily becomes more efficient, more profitable, and more fulfilling for its individual members.

It is my intent for you, reading this book, is that the Psyched On Service Mentality will facilitate both an examination of your own thinking in addition to the way your fellow employees think about business; in general and in your business specifically. If we want to enroll our employees in the Psyched On Service Mentality, it's time to answer an important question: WHAT'S IN IT FOR THEM?

WHAT MOTIVATES YOUR PEOPLE

Know Thy Employee
A Few Words from the Experts, THEM!

It's been said that we cannot motivate anyone, that we can only create an environment in which they may motivate themselves. Great observation but where's the beef? What is it that motivates them in the first place? Perhaps with this in mind we can then get down to the part of creating that environment thing.

A study by the United States Chamber of Commerce compared the thoughts of employees and the thoughts of their supervisors on performance motivation. 40,000 employees were asked to rank a list of ten motivators (given below) in order of the importance to them. 5,000 supervisors were asked to rank the same list in the order they thought *their employees* would rank them.

THE TEN MOTIVATORS	Employee	Supervisor
1) Full appreciation of the work done.	3	7
2) Feeling "in" on things.	4	8
3) Sympathetic help on personal problems.	9	10
4) Job security.	2	1
5) Good wages.	1	2
6) Work that keeps you interested.	6	6
7) Promotion and growth in the company.	5	3
8) Personal loyalty to workers.	8	5
9) Good working conditions.	7	4
10) Tactful discipline.	10	9

In each case, the first number given is the rank given by employees and the second number is the rank given by their supervisors. Four motivators in particular bear commentary.

While they were pretty much in synch on the first two motivators, good wages and job security, there is a surprising disparity between the next two motivators as ranked by employees and their supervisors. Perhaps the most striking finding of the study is the apparent disconnect in awareness of supervisors on just how important feelings of involvement and feelings of being appreciated are to their employees' motivation. Imagine how much more productive these workers would be if those needs were met. Unsatisfied needs are a true energy drain and the solution here costs literally nothing. An acknowledgement, an update is a small price to pay in that fix.

There are too many books out there to help those who are in need of specific strategies to do these two important managerial job functions. While most of them are common sense, it doesn't hurt to get some other manager's common sense ideas from such books as Dr. Bob Nelson's book, <u>1001 Ways to Reward Employees</u>, and <u>1001 Ways to Energize Employees.</u>

So you want to be a success, eh?
Perhaps the greatest definition of success that I've come across is as follows:

> *Success is not having to work with buttheads, knuckleheads & dirtbags. This is a concept that I and a former partner*

and I came up with many years ago while vacationing in Maui. The next day I thought that it might have been the wine that caused us to think it was so brilliant. But you know some 15 years later that definition still holds up. Success is not having to work with buttheads. Going further with that success might be defined as the opportunity and honor of working with other professionals; the opportunity of working with good people. That's as good a definition as I've found. So how successful are YOU right now? Do you want to be? What are you willing to do? What are you willing to NOT do? Who are you willing to associate with and who are you willing to disassociate with?

Are you one of those people who are a pleasure to work with, one who fits that definition of success? Hmmmmmmm

In subsequent chapters, we will explore ways of identifying & becoming these people.

ADAPTABILITY

How not to get left behind, or kicked there

Without hard work, you can't succeed. That's been the unwritten motto of American professionals since 1776. You know that. Your father told you that. Or your mother did. It's one of those things that everybody knows. And, you know what? It's absolutely true.

What most people don't know is this: success is not only about working hard. It's about working smart. And working smart is about adaptability.

Today's professional, now more than ever faces a competitive marketplace. And the competition is not to expend the maximum amount of effort, but to get the best and the most cost-effective results.

You could ride a horse to work. You could communicate with clients by telegram. You could ignore the technology revolutionizing every industry. But unless your boss is Gene Autry or you're living in the nineteenth century, you're going to get

left behind, living in a log cabin right next to the freeway.

There's a technological dimension to success in every industry that's increasingly hard to ignore. Being adaptable means viewing the changing technology not as a threat to your way of doing business, but as an opportunity to expand the services you provide and to find and delight new customers. Clearly, change manifests in other areas than technical methods, systems, and brands.

Take eye doctors as an example. Think about the Lasik laser surgery procedure. The advent of the laser as a medical instrument is just one reminder. If you keep your nose to the grindstone, you might look up one day and discover no one's using grindstones anymore.

The technology of every industry is changing fast. And adapting to change is an essential core function of your job, no matter what it is. Further, the core competence of every business is adaptability. That goes for any business in any industry, from computers to optometry to fast food. When was the last time you went to McDonald's and there wasn't something new on the menu?

It never was your way of doing business. It's their way of doing business. Adaptability means being ready to give customers what they want. The Lasik procedure is not popular because optometrists like it. The Lasik procedure is popular because clients do. A company incapable of responding to its customers' needs, whims, and wants is dead. It's that simple.

Knowing that is the first key to success. And any professional prepared to adapt, to meet the needs of the consumer is at a major advantage in his job and in the job market.

We've been DUPED.

We were taught in school "Survival of the _____*.   * *(Fittest)*

We were duped, big time. Remember that the Tyrannosaurus Rex was pretty fit if you look at the drawings. They didn't exactly survive. There was a time that Admiral Television was fit and so was Kaypro Computer. They aren't around. There are scores of companies, teams, organizations and nations that at one time were quite fit... and they're not around anymore.

Seems today, with the rate and pace of change, the we ought to teach a wholesale modification to read, "Survival of the _____*

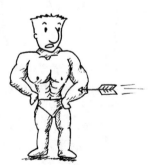

Fittest

Most Flexible

* *(Most Flexible, Most Adaptable).*

For example:

The National Wooden Blankety Blank Association (name changed in part to protect the identity) exists to further the agenda of its constituent members. These are the folks that manufacture and distribute blankety blanks, that which goods and products are shipped in and on (oops, I slipped). I addressed their convention early in my career and in doing so needed to have a bunch of research to feel confident to speak in front of these fine folks. The biggest challenge they had was that there was a tremendous shortage of wood back then (not that its in abundance today!). There was an alternative material offered, which was an artificial material and therefore other wood. This alternative material was largely rejected because, as they said, " We are the National <u>Wooden</u> Blankety Blank Association and had been for years. You can't be suggesting we go to an alternative material. We've distributed wooden pallets for years. It's all about wood! It always has been and always will be!" Good argument except for one thing.... there aint no wood. Unfortunately for some of them, it was too late to make the shift from wood to an alternative manmade material. The resistance to change sent them back too far. Our suggestion to them, to embrace the *possibility of a new material, or to at least consider it, was quite simple. (and they said that it really worked) Simply put, we advised that they change positions and argue in favor of the new material. Think of all of the reasons why to make the changes and argue for them vehemently. This helps to keep an open mind and prevent that dreaded disease Psychosclerosis.... aka hardening of the attitudes!*

Lighten up for greater results

Humor is the greatest productivity enhancer that I've ever found and used. We can get down right dead serious during the day and that aint called that by accident. The more serious we are without humorous reprise, detours to lighter, happier thoughts, the closer we become to 'buying the farm'. In fact, my friend Peter McLaughlin, in his book, <u>Catchfire</u>, gives perhaps the best treatise on the importance of laughter and mirth in the workplace and how it impacts productivity and effectiveness. I was so glad to read that book. It gave me an excuse to have fun in the workplace and to do so in the name of productivity enhancement. Because it is my nature to be playful, this was a great find. Also, I recall reading that **there is an inverse correlation between tension and retention.** If that is true, and I believe it is because it comes from the work of Bob Pike in his epic book, Creative Training Techniques, then it gives me the excuse to have fun in my trainings and keynotes. After all, it is my job to make certain that the messages are retained and that only happens when tension is reduced often thru laughter and fun. Hence, my license to shtick!

Harry Paul, co-author of FISH! A Remarkable Way To Boost Morale, and I have collaborated for many years on different ways that organizations create and maintain high performing cultures. His must read book, FISH! is a great way to expose and enlist co-workers in the process of workplace productivity thru proactive levity. Our conclusion on the topic is really quite simple; an environment of fun and a general sense of en"joy"ment at the workplace yields greater dividends. Employees who understand their role in the mission, who are working toward personal and professional growth and who have the associated positive self esteem will be more and more productive when unencumbered with the unnecessary fears and stress of the super serious environment. I am hoping that those of us who appreciate this can communicate it to those who believe that the workplace is no place for fun, that fun is the middle name of dysfunction and should be avoided or only allowed temporarily.

JOB SECURITY

How to get it, when it's not available in stores.

People want job security. Dogs and cats could care less about the subject, but if you're a human being, chances are you've given the matter some thought, whether you're working in the mailroom or in the big corner office.

One of the tall tales of American professional life is that job security is synonymous with the American Way. Many of us grew up with a Norman Rockwell painting in our heads: a man gets hired out of school; he goes to work for General Electric, works for about fifty years, gets a gold watch and a handshake, and promptly moves to Florida.

There are two problems with that picture. One, they have bugs in Florida the size of Cadillacs. Two, if job security like that ever existed, it has gone forever. In today's job market, fifty years ago is ancient history.

PSYCHED ON SERVICE

Business today operates at a speed few people could have predicted twenty or even ten years ago, leaving you just enough time to curse the fax machine before cutting short your frozen dinner. Your job can now follow you home.

Beyond the new technology, business practices are changing just as fast. We live in an age of downsizing and globalization. If you want a good job, start a temp agency.

And if you think the changes are over, you're kidding yourself. Today's computers are abacuses compared to what's coming. And considering the shift in global commerce, it might be a good time to brush up on your Chinese.

You've read the bumper stickers. Shift happens... especially today, all-day, faster and faster. I can recall vividly that as a psych counselor at SUNY Buffalo, way back in 1977, that there was a stress epidemic of grand proportion. Much of the stress seemed to stem from the pace and rate of change. That was way, way before even the first Personal Computers were readily available. They thought change was rampant then? Compare job functions, job responsibilities and new skills and behaviors required, mergers, acquisitions, downsizing, rightsizing. In this

context, I love to ask audiences if there is such a thing as job security.

Their answer: a resounding NO.
I then ask them if job security is something that people want and strive for? Their answer: ABSOLUTELY. And they are 100% correct. There's the rub. People want to reduce the stress of job insecurity and fundamentally believe that there is no such thing.
My offer to them and to you is to gift you the time tested and immutable principles that lead to job security and the resultant self-esteem, liberty and confidence that come with it. After all, who's more interested in your job security than you? No one. The good news is: you can do it.
Sounds simple, but how?

The Two Pillars of Job Security

1. The first rule is to choose an industry and team that are moving forward. You want a forward-moving company in a forward-moving industry. The vinyl records industry is not the place for you. Bagels trump donuts. And if your company sells typewriters, the unemployment office is right down the hall from Social Security.
There's no way around it. Competition in today's marketplace is tough. As a working professional, your choice of organization is

<u>critical</u>. It matters where you work. Your job description is not a laundry list of things to do. Your job is to help your company succeed. A company on the move in an evolving industry is in the right place and the only place you'll find job security. That's half of the equation and, by the way, the easier half.

2. Here is the other half. A thriving company needs thriving people. Job security comes from being the right person for the job. The trick is *becoming that person.* It is as simple as analyzing your core job functions carefully. What is it that you do that contributes to your productivity, your accomplishment of job functions, and your success? Get really naked with yourself (c'mon, I mean stripped of ego and false illusion, not skivvies) and take an honest inventory of your skills and abilities as they relate to becoming the excellent employee for you and your firm. Then, in all honesty, rate yourself on a scale from 1-10, with 10 being mastery and 0 being "duh". From "Duh" to "Cha ching". Simple, right? Easy, no! Then, with this honest audit, make certain plans to close the disconnects. If you are a 6 on managing multiple tasks and commit to being an 8 within 4 months, then plan your work and work your plan. That's called PGA and it has nothing to do with golf. It's **Performance GAP Analysis**; analyze the current reality, commit to a heightened performance level and plot a course of action to close the gap from 6 to 8 in 4 months. Then get on with it. As you take action you are taking action toward job security.

How do you think it feels to take this action? You already know how it feels. It's awesome. It invokes what is referred to as the Law of Control.

> **Law of Control** – we feel good about ourselves to the extent that we are in control of our time, our lives. Our self-esteem is in proportion to our feeling in control of our lives.

The opposite is true as well. We feel out of sorts, our self-esteem takes a major hit when we feel out of control.

Anyone who works off of lists can tell you how good it feels to check off something that you've accomplished. I mean it's a rush, isn't it?

> *How many of us do this: we accomplish something that is not yet on the list, we put it on the list after it is accomplished just so we can get the rush of positive energy when we check it off? Yes?*

From the point of view of the business manager, our new understanding of job security gives you a powerful incentive for enrolling employees in the Psyched On Service Mentality. And there's no correlation between "smarts", intelligence and job security...

in·tel·li·gence
Pronunciation: in-'te-l&-j&n(t)s
Function: *noun*
Etymology: Middle English, from Middle French, from Latin *intelligentia,* from *intelligent-,* *intelligens* intelligent
Date: 14th   century
1 a (1) : the ability to learn or understand or to deal with new or trying situations : **REASON**; *also* : the skilled use of reason (2) : the ability to apply knowledge to manipulate one's environment or to think abstractly as measured by objective criteria (as tests) **b** *Christian Science* : the basic eternal quality of divine Mind **c** : mental acuteness

*A former business partner and mentor of mine, speaker/ author Brian Tracy, reminded me that academic credentials aren't necessarily the litmus test of intelligence. He's one of the brightest people I have ever known... and at the time we were together, he himself wasn't, in the words of Zig Ziglar, "encumbered with a lot of college degrees". He was spot right as he described **intelligence** not as a way of thinking but rather as a way of behaving. He suggested that if one sets* *goals and acts in a manner consistent with the achievement of those goals that that is a true sign of intelligence. Thus, everything done in support of those goals is smart and everything done that moves you away from those goals is stupid. Sound too simple? At first, it sounded that way to me, but after thinking about it made sense. Now, some 10+years later, it still holds up as true. Sometimes I catch myself doing some downright stupid things. Happily, I catch myself fairly often. If I don't though I can always count on my wife to catch me, she's a pro at it.*

TRY IT ON YOURSELF.

The concept of Performance GAP Analysis is nothing new or earth shattering. It is, however, a most powerful tool to monitor your current reality, set goals, and close the disconnect between the two. It's not magic. We do it every day intuitively. For example, your kid has a fever of 101.6°F. Your obvious goal is 98.6°F. Your Performance GAP Analysis shows a differential of 3°F and your actions are in the complete direction of closing the gap. One can pretty much do the same methodology on each job function that we perform, each parental task…and on and on.

What are two areas in your life that you want to evaluate and "close the gap" using Performance GAP Analysis?

Action Planner

Professional Goal:

Stated in the present tense: i.e. I read 3 books per month in my professional field.

_____

_____

_____

_____

My personal evaluation of my present situation, on a scale of 1 (incompetence) – 10 (mastery) is _____.

My desired competency, on a scale of 1 (incompetence) – 10 (mastery) by 30 days is

_____.

The Performance GAP is _____.

My plan to close the gap involves:

1. _____

2. _____

3. _____

4. _____

Personal Goal

Stated in the present tense: i.e. I read 3 books per month in my professional field.

_____

_____

_____

_____

My personal evaluation of my present situation, on a scale of 1 (incompetence) - 10 (mastery) is _____.

My desired competency, on a scale of 1 (incompetence) – 10 (mastery) by 30 days is

_____.

The Performance GAP is _____.

My plan to close the gap involves:

1. _____

2. _____

3. _____

4. _____

Family Goal

Stated in the present tense: i.e. I read 3 books per month in my professional field.

_____

_____

_____

_____

My personal evaluation of my present situation, on a scale of 1 (incompetence) – 10 (mastery) is _____.

My desired competency, on a scale of 1 (incompetence) – 10 (mastery) by 30 days is _____.

The Performance GAP is _____.

My plan to close the GAP involves:

1. _____

2. _____

3. _____

4. _____

If you want more goal setting exercises, I highly recommend you secure Gary Blair's book, <u>What Are Your Goals?</u> It is a fantastic, self paced program to assist you thru your goals on all levels. Rather than preach the importance of setting goals, Gary assists you with psychologically stimulating questions in a workbook format that many of my clients have found useful – for themselves and their team. It worked for me.

Chapter 2

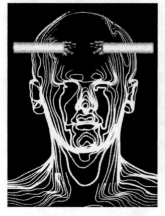

DISCONNECTS & SYNAPSES

DISCONNECT ONE:
Employees are not educated about their role in the business' marketing plan.

SYNAPSE ONE:
Upholding the credibility and reputation of the company by employee actions.

DISCONNECT TWO
Business ignores or mismanages marketing opportunities with customers.

SYNAPSE TWO:
Making the most of all available marketing opportunities.

DISCONNECT THREE:
Business overestimates the value of its product or service in its marketing plan.

SYNAPSE THREE:
Providing the customer with a positive emotional experience.

DISCONNECT FOUR:
Business has no strategy to recover from mistakes, mishaps, and errors.

SYNAPSE FOUR:
Learning the art of damage control.

DISCONNECT FIVE:
Front-line employees are not taught the communication skills they need to be effective.

SYNAPSE FIVE:
Applying the science of interpersonal communication.

DISCONNECT ONE:

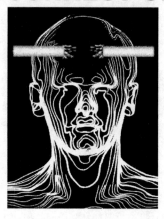

Employees are not educated about their role in the business' marketing plan.

Don't break your chickens before they hatch.
Every company in the Forbes, Fortune, Inc., and Fast Company 500 have a marketing department. That's no surprise to anyone. But, besides recruiting a horde of college-age assassins to get you to switch long-distance plans, what does the marketing department do?

They go to trade shows. They acquire client lists. They take surveys and research the demographics for company products. They prepare charts, show them at meetings, and imply the world will end if somebody doesn't increase the advertising budget.

But before anything else, the marketing department has one job: create a good

30

impression. It's up to the marketing department to present the company to consumers in the best possible light. Would you rather go to a Health Center or a Disease Clinic? When they think of you and your dependability, do you invoke your desired response? Do you know how you are regarded, how they respond to you? Controlling the impressions of the consumer is a vital part of business.

Every company, regardless of the product it sells or the service it provides, is a brand. Our associations for that brand are more powerful than they may first appear. Even some of the best-known and seemingly indestructible brand names can self-destruct. There will be no more Oldsmobiles, because the brand failed to transition to a younger demographic. Is there anything wrong with an Oldsmobile? Not necessarily. But the brand is broken. The car sounds old, not classic. And in the auto industry old is obsolete.

The influence of marketing is ubiquitous in every industry. Much more than at any other time in history, we are living in the Age of Marketing, aka the age of **impression management**. For this reason, it is stupefying to realize that for all the billions of dollars that go into marketing, all the slick ads and research studies, many companies continue to get it wrong. They do not educate their employees about **their** role in the business' marketing plan... the all-important role of managing impressions with each and every interaction they have with the world.

The marketing department, such as we traditionally know it, ultimately has limited control over the customers' impression of the company. The moment of truth comes when the customer meets the front-line employee: when she asks the doctor's receptionist for help with the insurance forms, when she requests new silverware from the waiter, when she complains to the restaurant manager about the waiter's lousy service, when she asks for some help carrying her groceries, or when she asks the sales clerk for a Kleenex. How gracefully and generously the response comes makes a huge difference in the customer's attitude towards not just the employee in question but towards the entire company. A bad impression is hard to erase.

I submit to you that every bank branch, every dentist's office, and every plant nursery has a marketing department. So does every taco stand in Southern California. It is every employee's job to make the right impression, as they are the most important member of the marketing team every day all day.

The next chapter will deal with how to make that happen.

SYNAPSE ONE

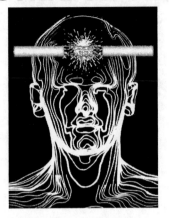

Upholding the credibility and reputation of the company.

Congratulations, you've got a new job in marketing.

As business managers, how do we educate our employees about their role in our company's marketing plan? The first step is obvious, but it takes guts. It takes leadership. It takes strength and determination. It takes certain unmentionable parts of the anatomy; and, in business, they're not just for the boys.

Everything starts at the top. The business manager has got to enroll each and every member of team in a new program of excellence, to let them know they are now members of the marketing department with a brand new title: Associate Marketer.

Let them know: "Every hour you're at work, every interaction with every customer, every patient, every client, every vendor, you are on display."

They are on stage all day. There's a company just north of our San Diego office that generates billions of dollars and pleases millions of customers every year... and it is based on the identity of a <u>rodent</u>. Got it yet – It's Disneyland. They knew earlier than most that their employees, every last one of them, are on stage and being observed. Walt knew that each employee was basically a cast member – and that's what he called them then and that's what they are called today. Letting your people know that they are being observed on a regular basis by their customers, their families, and basically, everyone need not be a paranoia inducing observation. It can and, I argue, must be a consciousness building experience.

Look, it may not be part of your job to inspire excellence, but it could be. Inspire them by "afflicting them" as we discussed earlier. You don't have to hop up on the conference table for a locker-room speech. On the other hand, if you do, give me a call. I'd love to see it.

But we're not after theater. We're after open lines of communication. And the first thing to communicate is this: the company is creating new standards of conduct. As Associate Marketers, it is now part of every employee's job to uphold the credibility and reputation of the company. In addition, remember, keeping this at the front of their mind is a selfish thing for every employee to master. Why, because it gives them the assurance that they are closing the gap on the essential job function of customer service which in turn adds to their job security. A Successfully Selfish Servant. Sounds good.

Have this tattooed across the receptionist's forehead: To uphold the credibility and reputation of the company. Stencil it on the company car. It is now the motto of the marketing department and every one of us is in the marketing department every minute of every day.

Make it clear that when we vent our frustrations on the customer, when we act unprofessionally, when we argue with our coworkers, when we talk down another department, we aren't just damaging the customer's perception of us, but the credibility and reputation of the entire company. The customer doesn't think that you stink; they think that the whole place reeks.

Only by holding ourselves to the highest possible standards can we avoid the trap of mediocrity. In addition, mediocrity is **contagious**. Let's be clear here. This is not an

invitation to be a dictator. This is not a denunciation of fun. Far from it. By all means, be friendly. Be all means, have a sense of humor. We are not looking for robots. We are looking for professionals. We are talking about providing the customer with a positive emotional experience. That's the distinguishing characteristic between organizations that thrive and those that exist. Every time we succeed in doing that, we're advertising ourselves. We are making an investment in the company's credibility and reputation.

If mediocrity is contagious, then excellence is infectious. If you make an effort to enlist your employees' help, if you create an atmosphere of team pride, if you make it a conscious goal to uphold the credibility and reputation of the company, I think you'll find a few steps in the right direction will get you almost all the way home. Without that essential synapse, you're sunk.

Where Ma Bell blew it.

I had the opportunity of working with some of the executives of a telecommunications company, which will remain anonymous for the purpose of this point. Their initials are AT&T. That should cloak them well.

Anyway, they had a brand identity that was associated with warm, fuzzy feelings. Many of us can remember how "Ma Bell" advertised their soft motherly relationship on television just about every day. Their ads included a son calling home from college only to hear his mom say "you never call." And his response was "but Momma, I am calling." Touching the heart of us all, in a manner that we can relate to... it was a very successful button that they pressed in us to perpetuate the "Ma" in "Ma Bell."

Competitors would call us and try to seduce us away from our motherly relationship with "Ma." Our collective response to their overtures was a resounding, NO THANKS. "Ma" had taught us well.

Then, after these aggressive competitors tried a different approach- undercutting price – or so they claimed, what did "Ma" say? She pointed her finger with animosity and said, reeled out in a tone that we hadn't ever heard "Ma" speak in, "MAKE THEM PUT IT IN WRITING."

"'Ma', you don't talk that way. What's going on? That's not our 'Ma'." And they broke the bond that bond that they worked so hard to establish. They changed the fundamental basis of our relationship. AND BROKE THE BOND.

The *God Only Knows* Factor

We came across an interesting study that offers a fascinating explanation of customer bonding and client relationships.

In this study, they asked thousands of customers why they bought from whom they bought.

The group was divided into three categories:

Group 1. Features and Benefits- they selected and stayed with their vendor because of the features and benefits such as two pair of eyeglasses for $99.

Group 2. Relationship – these people claim that they purchased from whom they purchased based upon feeling a relationship they perceived with the vendor.

Group 3. This group, the LARGEST group, stated in response to the question, why do you buy from whom you buy? answer, "God Only Knows!" They had no idea why they chose that vendor and why they stay with that vendor.

The next question posed of these people was, "Would you switch?"

Herein lies the great lesson.

Group 1. Features and Benefits- said, "absolutely, we'd switch."

Group 2. Relationship – these people also said that they would switch if presented with the right circumstances."

Group 3. God Only Knows group, the LARGEST group, when asked if they'd switch stated, "NO WAY!"

Something, some mysterious voodoo mojo, occurred between these folk and their vendor that bonded them like superglue. We call that the God Only Knows factor (GOK factor).

For example, the Ma Bell GOK factor was that emotional connection that we had with "Ma". Too bad that they broke that bond with the "Make them put it in writing" campaign.
To the best of our ability of understanding it we, at David Corbin's Performance Technology Group, believe our GOK factor to be our demonstrable concern for the success of our clients; that we observe and opine on all contributing aspects of their business success and have the conviction to share even if it is not so politically correct to do so.

What is **your** GOK factor? What could it be? Why do people stay with your company and your deliverables?
When you find out **your** GOK factor, guard it, nurture it, train on it and value it as an essential asset of your company.

CONTINUOUS PERSONAL IMPROVEMENT

How to be indispensable in a temporary job market

Good job! You made it to the first synapse. I want you to ask yourself a question: Who's the right person for your job? You are.

And let's keep it that way. Job security depends on continuous self-evaluation and Continuous Personal Improvement. I love the title of Intel CEO Andy Grove's book, <u>Only The Paranoid Survive</u>. He argues in favor of what we've been discussing here, that we are obtusely introspective and continuously consider our position in the marketplace, in the world. How do we fare against the expectations of the job, the marketplace, and the world?

A previous chapter remarked on the necessity of becoming the right person for the job. Now it's time to be specific. How do you become the right person for your job?

Start simply. Take some time and inspect what you are expected to do. What's expected of you at work each day? Ask yourself, "What do my employers and co-workers expect of me? What do my partners expect of me? What do

my clients, patients or customers depend on
me to do?"
Be very specific.
We're after the actual day-to-day duties of
your job. If you were an X-Ray Technician,
you might list the following:

1) develop X-Rays
2) maintain machinery
3) notify doctors when X-Rays are ready
4) keep records
5) ...

> It's not enough to be good in
> most things and lousy in one.
> It doesn't seem to all fit
> together... as above.

And so on. You could probably list at least a
dozen if you tried. Make your own list.
Be thorough. There's more to every profession
than any outsider would think. Contrary to
popular opinion, bankers don't know a hell of
a lot about swinging a wrecking ball. Even
marketing types don't know everything. It's up
to you, with consultation of others if
necessary, to decide exactly what it's your job
to do. Now you've got a list of maybe ten
expected everyday duties. We could call these
your job's "core functions."

Take the first item on your list. Think of one concrete way you could improve your job performance in this area.

   1) read wrecking ball manual

Take a minute and go down your list one item at a time.

   2) don't wreck foreman's Porsche again

Some areas will be stronger than others. But hopefully you've discovered some ways your job performance could be improved.

If not, we've got a problem. There is always room for improvement, even for the most successful companies and the brightest, most competent people. You never have it perfect and you shouldn't want to. Because the best way of doing business and the best way to do your job is always changing.

Lessons from WOODSTOCK

You probably don't remember reading in my dedication of this book the reference to Max Yasgur. He was the owner of the land on which the original Woodstock Festival was held in August 1969. Well kind reader, this author was there at the age of 16 years old. (If my kid asked to attend such an event I'd give her a whack on the noggin...) but at age 16 I took leave of my sleep away camp summer job to attend that historic event. It was unreal, life changing and, at many levels, extremely educational. Believe that.

The single greatest lesson I took away from Woodstock was more than the survival lessons or the political statement of a nation's youth. Rather it came from the mouth of a Zen, mystic, very, very stoned individual who when we asked if he needed help (he was so zoned we didn't know if he was in crisis, trauma or nirvana). He told us that he was contemplating a concept that he just read in a book. He then said, and I quote, actually I quote it often,

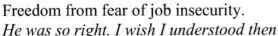

"Hey Man, like you're either Green and Growing... or Ripe and Rotting." Continuous Improvement yields Personal Confidence, Heightened Self Esteem, Personal Liberty and Freedom from fear of job insecurity.

He was so right. I wish I understood then what I do now about the wisdom of that statement. Happily, I realize the profundity of that quip.

*I teach, I believe, I know that we are indeed either **Growing or Rotting but***

never, ever standing still in business or in life.

In business and professional life, you are either green and growing or ripe and rotting. There is no middle ground.

You have the never-ending opportunity to find a better way of doing business. The chance to learn is always available to you! Take advantage of it, because the better you do your job, the more you'll get out of it and the closer you'll stand to job security.

The more you know about your job, your organization, your way of doing business, the more valuable you become. Learning is not wasted effort. It's within your power to make yourself indispensable to your company. If for some reason your company does not recognize your skills or if some unforeseen occurrence causes the demise of your company and you are let go... no problema. Now, with your confidence and competence, you simply do what that great business philosopher and personal development guru, Frank Sinatra, sez and "just pick yourself up and get back in the race, cause THAT'S LIFE!"

Performance GAP Analysis and Personal Offered with apologies to the college funds of the Psychiatric community.

Chapter 3
DISCONNECT TWO:

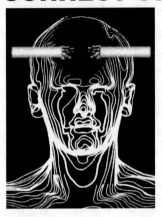

**Business ignores or mismanages marketing
opportunities with customers.**

Welcome to the money factory.
Radical though it may seem, most businesses
and most people are interested in making
money. With some people, the need to make
money is pathological. We call them greedy.
A chosen few could care less about money.
We call them monks. A small segment of the
population is spectacularly good at making
money. We call them rich, at least financially.
And if the rich ones are telling jokes at the
lunch meeting, call them hilarious. They might
just get you a raise.

The point is, we all know business is about
making money. Or that's what we thought. The

real truth is, business is about making the most money you possibly can without ending up in jail or the subject of Third World protest. And some of us are flexible on the second point.

It's about maximizing profit. Such remarks have occasioned many eloquent men and women to once again comment: Duh. But if that's so obvious, why do we such a bad job of it? It seems a straightforward objective. It is a straightforward objective. But somewhere along the way, we tend to get lost.

I've written elsewhere in this book about the routinization of our jobs. Everybody has experienced this to some extent. Your job becomes routine. Your life becomes routine. You live and work on autopilot.

Businesses do the same. The auto parts store begins to think of itself as an auto parts store, instead of what it really is: a moneymaking factory. Every business has a core competence, an expertise. Specialization is a necessary part of business. It's an equally inexcusable error for a business to drift away from what it's good at, the products and services on which it built its reputation. But we cannot allow ourselves to do business in such a routine way that we cease to innovate in the ways we bring in income. The business ignores or mismanages marketing opportunities with customers. Ask yourself these questions: what have we done and what can we do to address the marketing potential of our daily interactions with customers in person and through other media?

To clarify, when the customer's attention is available to you, in your place of business or on the telephone or through a newspaper ad or at a trade show, what are you doing to maximize the marketing value of that interaction?

The next chapter will continue to address this central problem and will suggest some possible solutions.

SYNAPSE TWO:

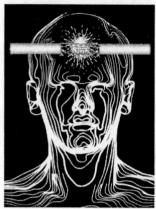

Making the most of all available marketing opportunities.

How do you sell pizza to a teenager?
If the pet rock has taught us anything, it's that there's always an opportunity to make more money. If the supermarket check stand has taught us anything, it's group your impulse-oriented luxury items in an attractive display by the register because people are essentially slaves to their own immediate gratification.

The previous chapter introduced the second major internal marketing mistake to which most companies are susceptible. The business ignores or mismanages marketing opportunities with customers.
Take the auto parts store. A man takes his car to the auto parts store to buy a new air filter. He goes up to register with his new air filter. He waits in line behind the guy with the

muffler bracket for a 69 Datsun, looking around at... nothing! Empty space. A marketing void. The auto parts store could do a lot with that space, but they've chosen the wonderfully insane alternative of... nothing! Fill that space with bumper stickers, air fresheners, and driving gloves. Put something there. The point is the auto parts store could take a page from the grocery store.

In fact, there is no real reason the auto parts store couldn't sell gum and candy bars and magazines, just like the grocery store. Now it bears pointing out that many auto parts stores probably do just that. Smart corporations discover ways to make money. But I'll bet you can find one that doesn't.

Take IKEA. If you've never been, the Swedish-based home furnishing retailer is huge. If there weren't big friendly yellow arrows on the floor, some of us would still be wandering around among the dinette sets looking for a way out. Is it an accident that halfway through the place, just when you're about to faint, there's a Swedish cafeteria? Of course not. It's brilliant marketing.

The principle of opportunistic marketing is not limited to traditional retailers. Recently, I consulted with one of the largest and most successful medical groups in the country, particularly with their optometric outfit. And every facility I went to I noted a large display case in the lobby, filled with their available eyewear. I'll say it again. Brilliant marketing. The case is there as a reminder: in case you've forgotten, after you get your prescription, buy your glasses here. Buy your contacts here. Buy your prescription sunglasses here. You've got them in the building, so sell them something.

When your clients wait on hold, are they listening to Vivaldi or to "50% off all home fumigations!"? Just an idea. I've got nothing against Vivaldi. But the point is that companies have more marketing opportunities than they realize and a wider range of weapons than they choose to use.

Now examples like these or the principles behind them may very well have occurred to you before. I don't doubt it. But chances are, you can think of some way to take advantage of marketing opportunities your company has missed. The issue here is to get yourself floating ideas, to get a whole office full of Associate Marketers throwing out ideas.

How do sell pizza to a teenager?   Offer him some.

Learn to enjoy the process of self-improvement. Applying these the ideas of this book, really trying for Continuous Personal Improvement is a philosophy of success, an attitude towards the future, and a practical program for change. Now that you've made it to synapse number two, let's take a little breather as in the next two chapters we

continue to examine the practical side of pro-
active change.

Yet another example of innovative marketing
that we've come across is:

*There's an event ticket that was trying to
compete with TicketMaster and TicketTron
and all the big companies. Their break
through idea is about follow-up. What they
did was simple. After a concert, they call
up and ask you how you enjoyed the show.
This gives you an opportunity, as a patron,
to give feedback while at the same time it
gives them an opportunity to ask, " by the
way if there is anything else we can do for
you would you please let us know." Then
they commence to discuss some of the
programs scheduled in that area in the
near future. This simple follow-up system
contributed to radically increased market
share, which has been going up month, by
month, by month to their delight.*

Innovation at it's finest

Could you imagine a software program and
methodology that will take a look at your
problem and offer you fresh ways of looking
at that issue? Now, what if that model makes
recommendations to you based upon hundreds
and thousands of other such challenges and
how those challenges were dealt with which

then culminated in such originality as to have been patentable? It is available today and it doesn't cost a zillion dollars. The process is called TRIZ, an acronym for continuous improvement in the Russian language. Check out their website www.trizjournal.com and see how Dr. Ellen Domb is helping companies large and small to innovate beyond their wildest dreams.

From ChangeVictim to ChangeMaster

*How to change when
you really don't want to.*

We could summarize the first forty thousand years of human philosophy in one sentence: change is bad. Fortunately, our culture has evolved a little since then. A little.

In one-way or another, we are all victims of habit. And the stranger and more ingrained our habits become, the harder they are to see. Like the old lady who moved to California, we put on our mittens every morning and then step outside to look for winter among the palm trees. I know it's December, but it's just not there.

Admit it. Ninety percent of your day is spent on autopilot; the morning shower, the cup of coffee, the commute to work, the pleasant hellos, the unpleasant ones, every single thing you do seems to do itself.

On a superficial level, maybe we should congratulate ourselves. As professionals, we're good at what we do. We train to do it. And before long we can do the job with our hands tied behind our backs. And with our backs tied to a 30-year mortgage.

Here's the problem. We can do more. In a previous chapter, we began to outline a program of Continuous Personal Improvement. If you were playing along, you listed the daily core functions of your job.

Change management might not have made your list, but it should have. Change is a part of your job. Managing change is a core function of your job.

By standing still, by doing the job the way we've always done it, we make ourselves victims of habit in more ways than one. By standing still, we not only don't improve ourselves, we slowly make ourselves obsolete.

We must foster in ourselves and in our coworkers a pro-active attitude towards change and towards the problems that necessarily arise in the working environment. In part, this issue is one of corporate culture and will be addressed in a later chapter. But the issue is not entirely outside of our control.

We can be the benefactors of habit and not the victims. We just need some new habits.

In every situation, we must assume that there is a positive course of action. Something can be done about our invoicing, about our declining revenues, about our slumping morale, about customer dissatisfaction.

Further, we can no longer be satisfied with reacting to problems as they arise. We must anticipate possible problem situations and act to prevent them or to minimize the damage.

There is more to your job than the papers waiting on your desk.

You will always have to fill out forms. Certain aspects of your job are not going to change. That's the curse of working. But you must not allow your thinking to become routine. A pro-active thinker is infinitely more valuable than a reactive one. You must strive to keep a fresh perspective on your working life, to reexamine your goals, to ask the difficult important questions: what could I be doing better and what could we be doing better?

Play for a winning team by helping your team win.

Managing the Process of Change

How to help yourself and everybody else too

Companies, like people, have bad habits. Every company needs protocols for how it conducts its business. Every company has its own routine. There's nothing wrong with that, but routinization is a dangerous thing. It can be lethal to your business. The individual professional's pro-active attitude will do him no good if his best ideas are diverted into the trash chute.

It is the responsibility of management to ensure that a free exchange of ideas is not only possible, but the norm. Let's be clear. There are and must be standards for professional conduct. An operating surgeon is the boss and her O.R. nurse or the head of her HMO has no business questioning the placement of her incision. On the other hand, the O.R. nurse has the right and the obligation to tell her she's about to sew up mean old Mrs. Robben with five pounds of gauze and a pair of forceps still inside her.

The situation might not be so drastic, but the secretarial pool really might know what they're talking about when they ask for the laser printer to be brought up from Subbasement Q22.

The lesson is this: whatever their position, respect people's competence to do their own job well and to know what they need to do it. In the end, they may not be right, but if you don't listen, you'll definitely be wrong.

Effective change management requires keeping an ear to the ground. A company that's attentive to its employees' concerns has a first-rate group of troubleshooters - a dream team of management consultants sitting in the lunchroom.

Beyond mere responsiveness, management must allow employees the freedom to take responsibility for their own self-improvement. A company's flexibility begins at the unit level. And the unit we're talking about is the individual professional. The rule is: where you can be flexible, be flexible. Makes sense, doesn't it? Overseeing every detail of your employees' work is not management; it's harassment.

By giving the individual a role in change management, a company simultaneously targets its problem areas with remarkable accuracy and gives an enormous boost to employee morale.

Effective change management does not end there. A company must invest in its employees. It's the only way to keep up with technology and competing business models. When management will not pay to train, mediocrity enters the system. And it's probably there to stay.

The truth is many companies do not manage change effectively. They will not pay to train on the new machinery or on the new software, fearing that every employee is itching to skip town with his expensive new training. But what's the alternative? Ultimately, it's a bunch of untrained employees without the tools to survive in a cutthroat marketplace.

Effective change management accounts for the necessity of continuous change. Every business is in constant transition. Employees are fired, hired, and retired. That's business as usual, but the employees you invest in will not only be better qualified to do their job but they're going to be happier and more effective knowing how much you value their expertise.

Learn to view every employee or every coworker as a human asset of the company. Not only that, every employee is an appreciating asset. Every day of experience and every increase in knowledge adds value to the individual professional. Any company that's in the game to win will realize it's an investment worth making.

On the flip side, the individual professional must be willing to invest his time in the company's success. Take every opportunity you have to train. It's a win-win value-added proposition. Your company gets a well-trained employee and you increase your worth not only to the company but also to the job market in general.

Empowering Questions

are very useful to ask yourself when you are in a reactive mode rather than a consciously aware and proactive mode. Often, under the influence of change or transition of life events, we revert to a state of daydreaming - a sort of sleep like state. This condition is driven by past associations to change and an attempt to divert our attention from that usually uncomfortable association. Essentially then, these probing questions change our mind's focus and therefore change our associated feelings and of course our autonomic responses to those feelings. By asking these questions, you stand a greater chance of staying awake and aware of the current situation or event. You will thus be able to create new associations to change that are, perhaps, more positive and less uncomfortable. Then, with each new change experience that you deal more effectively with, you stand a greater and greater chance of dealing with the change in the "here and now" of it.

1- What is the opportunity making itself available to me with this transition?
2- This is good. How can I benefit from this?
3- What have I done to deserve a wonderful opportunity such as this?

4- There is a great learning opportunity here for me. What could it be?

5- How has this has come to assist me in my personal development.

6- What is great about this change?

7- Why is it not perfect yet?

8- What am I willing to do to make it the way I want it?

9- What am I willing to no longer do to make it the way that I want it?

10-How can I enjoy the process while I do what is necessary to make it the way that I want it.

FORCE FIELD ANALYSIS

In order to manage a change in general, and the Resistance Phase in specific terms, we must first understand the change itself. In the late 1940's Dr. Kurt Lewin, generally regarded as the "father of change theory", developed a model for understanding change. This model is called Force Field Analysis and gives us an understanding of the forces pushing for or against a change.

The method is useful in breaking down a problem or an upcoming change into its basic components.

Identifying those key elements of the change about which something can realistically be done;

Developing a systematic strategy for problem solving or change implementation.

Creating the conditions for action planning.

Dr. Lewin suggested that in any given situation the behavior of an individual or group may be less than ideal. In order to move from "here" to "there", a particular activity level may be conceptualized as the product of a number of pressures or influences acting upon the individual, group, or organization. These influences are called forces and Lewin identified two major forces influencing behavior:

Driving Forces -
   Forces that move in the direction of the change.

Restraining Forces -
   Forces that move in the opposite direction of the change.

Since the two forces push in opposite directions, a point of balance is usually achieved which defines the status quo.

To alter these forces and thus influence behavior, Dr. Lewin suggests these three basic strategies for effecting change.

a. Add to the driving forces, which can strengthen the opposing forces and increase stress and tension. (it usually does!)

b. Add to the driving forces while reducing or eliminating the restraining forces.

c. Remove, or reduce restraining forces. (This is usually more desirable and practical, yet less obvious)

Idea:

Use the worksheet that follows to identify the driving forces, resisting forces, the desired goals, and the status quo. Next, discuss the best approach to accomplish the desired goals by reducing or eliminating the strength of the restraining forces.

Desired Goal: _____

Status Quo: _____

What is Driving Change?   *SQ

What are the resistors?   **DG

*Those Elements Pushing for the Change Effort

Those Elements Resisting the Effort

*SQ – Status Quo
**DG – Desired Goal

Create your own ChangeMasters

Many people know that there are few vinyl records being pressed today, that the medium of choice is the CD technology. Frankly, I don't think I'd want to hang my career on the future of the vinyl record business. Nor would I look to the typewriter industry for job security. Not a good choice you must agree. Clearly, like people, products change and innovate, are born and die and have their lifecycle. Some products are born, are ready for marketing but are obscured by the status quo and are thus not acknowledged as viable products for sales and marketing. Such was the case with the digital watch. Joel Barker, in his excellent videotape, Paradigms, makes this point so well that I will never forget it.

Apparently, the Swiss have been making watches for hundreds and hundreds of years. They employed tens of thousands of watchmakers. However, after the digital watch came out and became popular, the Swiss lost over two thirds of their business, their jobs and were devastated. Who put them out of business? It was Texas Instruments who took the digital watch to mass market. How did Texas Instruments come up with such innovation? They didn't. They bought it. From whom? Ready for this? They bought it from the Swiss, the same people that they annihilated in business. It was the Swiss who developed the digital watch but who dismissed it as being relatively useless. After all, they posed; it wasn't a threat to the watch business. It wasn't a real watch. It didn't even have any moving parts. So, they reasoned, let it go and let us continue on our path of watch making dominance. Big mistake. Texas Instruments observed it at a trade show, bought the rights to the technology and the rest is history... like many of the Swiss watch making jobs. Change requires that we keep our minds open to possibility.

Idea:

As a group, discuss some of the changes that are facing your industry. Capture these changes on a flipchart. Then, ask the group to discuss those changes that they really are not happy about. Make note of those on the flipchart. Next, have them break into groups and assign each group a different "unwanted change" to discuss in the following way:

They are to present to the group at large why this change is 'good', how it is beneficial to them and how it is such a gift to have occurred. There will be some rumbling, I can assure you. However, it is a great way to get the group looking at the change from a different perspective and to place on the table for clearer investigation many of the items that might otherwise get lost. This one can be a ton of fun.

Chapter 4
DISCONNECT THREE:

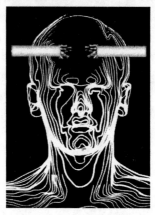

Business overestimates the value of its product or service in its marketing plan.

How do you choose an obstetrician with your eyes closed? Most of us would forgive a CPA for thinking it was his business to do other people's taxes. On the other hand, some of us who've been audited won't forgive him. Ever.

That's what we're taught. A CPA does your taxes. A plumber unclogs you sink. A waitress brings your food. Naturally, on some level, each of these statements is absolutely correct.

What's wrong with them is that they are fundamentally inadequate job descriptions. Sure enough, a CPA does your taxes, but is that really all it takes to be a successful accountant? Does a woman choose her obstetrician by reviewing mortality rates? Forgiving the morbid question,

the answer, usually, is no. A woman picks her sister's
obstetrician. She picks the obstetrician whose
office is closest to her home. She picks the obstetrician who has three children of her own. She picks a female obstetrician or a male one. She picks the nicest obstetrician. In short, she picks the obstetrician that makes her feel most comfortable, that inspires the most confidence, and that is most appealing to her as a person.

Ultimately, she will choose the obstetrician that seems the most capable over the one that is the most capable any day of the week. Not all of a consumer's decisions require the great care as a pregnant woman's choice of obstetrician. But we tend to choose according to the same emotional cues. The example serves to illustrate that there are a large number of peripheral issues to any decision and that these factors can be and often are preponderant in a consumer's decision.

In this example, we have the root of the third major internal marketing mistake that companies routinely make: The business overestimates the value of its product or service in its marketing plan. It's easy to see how this comes about. A CPA does your taxes. Well, then, an accounting firm does your credit union's taxes. A doctor treats the sick. Well, then, a hospital treats the sick.

From a marketing point of view, this is an inadequate representation. The next chapter will reassess the value of core products and services in the context of the Psyched on Service Mentality.

SYNAPSE THREE:

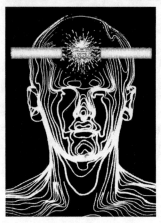

Providing the customer with a positive emotional experience.

Human beings, with an unfathomable capacity for analytical and deductive reasoning, are capable of believing that fifteen dollars worth of popcorn and Coca-Cola from the movie theater concession stand is less expensive than fifteen dollars of engine coolant from the local Jiffy Lube. Or at least their behavior suggests that they are. Fun is cheap, no matter how expensive it is.

This mystery is about two sentences long. We buy the things we like. As consumers, human beings are emotional creatures. Though at times necessity can bend us to a rational decision, in many ways, there is no rhyme and even less reason to the ways, we spend our money. Failure to consider the emotional needs and whims of the consumer is an incalculable error on the part of any company and a major contributing factor to the third major internal marketing error. The business overestimates the value of its product or service in its marketing plan.

David Gilman, ABOC, Director of Training at Kaiser Permanente So. Cal Vision Services tells this inspirational story.

"My next patient was an elderly lady who stated that her glasses were not working and wanted to return them for a refund. She seemed very upset and angry. It seemed that she was ready to start a hassle at any moment. I assured her that I would take care of her glasses to her satisfaction and excused myself to do just that. When I returned and had her try on the spectacles, she looked very fearful and distrusting. While she was able to see well at all distances, she was still very upset. I questioned her as to her reservations. She told me that she did not know what to do with her glasses, that her husband took care of all these kinds of things for her and then explained that he had just passed away last month. I touched her hand and expressed my sorrow for her loss. I further offered that if she had any future challenges with her eyewear that she should phone me personally and that I

would be pleased to be her 'eyeglass guy'. She cried with relief and happiness. She left happy and I was even happier to have helped her.

At the same time of this transaction, a young businessman was waiting for his turn with me and was listening in on the aforementioned conversation. He offered up that he really appreciated how I handled that interaction. He was very open with me about his eyewear needs and when it was all said and done he ended up ordering 4 pairs of glasses totaling about $1200.00.

I learned a very important lesson. From then on, I conducted my patient interactions as though I was being watched, as though I were on television. That helped me to stay present and behave in a way that would make my company and me very proud. After all, you never know who is watching. I knew that I was making myself an even more valuable employee so I made it a game to think that way. My confidence went up, my customer's satisfaction went sky high and so did mine!"

"Because I'm Worth It"
Demonstrating our worth.

Many of us are old enough to remember the perfume commercial that featured model Catherine Deneuve stating, "Buy me Chanel No. 5, because I'm worth it." Tough to argue because she is stunningly beautiful but clearly objective data, I think not.

So many businesses that produce high quality products are confronted with the challenge of justifying the initial investment fee associated with their deliverable. Put simply, they get the old price objection that we've all experienced. Companies like ResMed, the manufacturer of medical equipment for sleep breathing disorders, whose products are significantly better, more advanced and just add more value to the user, are often in a position of justifying their pricing structure. Distributors are so often tempted to take the path of least resistance and simply sell the less expensive priced units. What a shame. While you can't blame them for wanting to make the sale in less time, it is unfortunate to me, a user of this equipment, to not be offered the better product simply because the distributor can't or won't make the time to explain the value of the higher priced unit.

ResMed took this problem to task and came up with a positive solution that you might want to consider for your own application. They took the Return On Investment approach to the issue. They showed the distributor the dollars and cents implications of having to educate the patient, having to service and repair the equipment, technician time, follow-up visits and the like and factored that into the overall cost of doing business with them versus their competitors. Happily, ResMed's products are measurably more reliable, demonstrably easier to use and thus overall less expensive and more profitable to the distributor. Rather than just making big fat claims that their products are *better* and more *profitable*, they _showed_ that they are, in black and white and sometimes even in color. Again, bottom line, it works and everybody wins. The ROI method, try it.

The product or service a company provides is important. There's no mistaking that. Quality counts. But when the customer evaluates your company and your way of doing business, the quality of that service or product is one of many factors under consideration.
And it may not be top on the list. Quality is competing with reputation, and with cost, and with atmosphere, and with prestige, and with a

dozen other emotional factors that drive a customer's decision.

The most valuable part of a Rolls Royce is the hood ornament. That is not to say the Rolls Royce is not a quality car. But is it $200,000 better than a Honda? Even if the answer to that question is yes, it's clear that the Rolls Royce sells itself by its prestigious reputation.

Sticking with cars, in certain easily quantifiable ways, a Porsche Boxster is a considerably better car than a Geo Metro. It's faster. It's got better acceleration. It handles better. But a remarkable amount of its value can be attributed to the brand name associated with a particular piece of machinery.

If we refer back to Chapter 8, one of the Five Tenets of Marketing is to get the customer to like the product. or service as the case may be. In other words, it is our job to get her to associate a positive emotional experience with the product. We sure do want the customer to like the product, but the customer has got to like us.

It's about attitude. In 25 years of consulting, I've talked with people from all over the world and I've found that the core of every successful business relationship is attitude. Attitude decides the people we want to serve us, the colleagues we want to work with, the businesses we want to partner with, the employees we want to promote, and the bosses we want to work for. On the negative side, an attitude can decide the people we don't want to be in business with. In those 25 years my colleagues and I have given seminars in over 20 countries and to folks in about 8 different languages--a tremendously diverse sample of the world's work population. In many of those seminars, we asked essentially this question: what are the qualities of the people you want to work with? The answers broke down into two categories: skills and attitudes. Now, we know what a skill is: a learned competency in a particular task or group of tasks. And we know what an attitude is: an outlook on the world or an approach to dealing with others. The responses often looked like this:

ATTITUDES	SKILLS
Friendly Helpful	Product knowledge
Patient	Delegates
Hard working	Goal Oriented
Positive	Organized
Willing to go the extra mile	
Doesn't sweat the small stuff	
Takes the initiative	

Now that's an awful lot of attitude. Almost everywhere, we asked this question we noticed the same startling thing. Everywhere there was an 80/20 split between attitudes and skills. Eighty percent of our decision of whom we want to work with is based on the person's attitude. While we most often hire on the basis of skills, our professional relationships, whether between colleagues or between customer and employee, are formed on the basis of attitude. Internally, we promote on the basis of attitude and we fire on the basis of attitude. And externally the customer decides whom she's going to buy from on the basis of attitude.

What the business manager can do, what the business manager has got to do is inspire not only competent delivery of service, but an environment of excellence. That environment comes from teamwork. Build a team that surpasses every expectation of service that the customer may have. If you do that, the customer will come back. With three of her friends. In business, the extra mile is not extra; it is the necessary length to secure a customer's business, your company's longevity, and, finally, each and every employee's job security. Make it your company's philosophy that extraordinary service is not an arbitrary standard, but a component of success as necessary as advertising or the product itself.

THE FIVE TENETS OF MARKETING

Learning to do what you already know

Now that I've got a captive audience if I ever heard of one, I'm going to really talk to you about marketing.

You are now a marketing animal. Suffused with predatory awareness, you are now a shameless promoter of your own self-interest. There's nothing wrong with that. You're not being selfish. You're making the most out of yourself. The better you are at your job and the more aggressively you pursue success, the better for you and for everyone around you.

You are the uber-marketer, a suped-up internal combustion dynamo running on its own power and by its own initiative. A giant among mortals, a tiger among tomcats, a Muhammad Ali among Pee Wee Herman's.

Okay, enough of that. If you're reading this book, it's a good bet you've got the drive to succeed hard-wired into your brain. This book assumes you've got the motivation and more than a little know-how. We're not talking about the power supply; we're talking about the steering controls.

Having a Psyched on Service Mentality means keeping the principles of marketing in the forefront of your mind. ¡En la frente de la mente! It also means applying those principles to every situation.

> *A great example of keeping something in the front of your mind is when my daughter Jenna turned 16 while living in CA. Of course, 16 is the legal age to start driving. Anything and everything she did she related to driving. For example; if she took the garbage out she said, "See Daddy, I'm responsible. I took the garbage out I can drive." Or when she watched her brother, "See Daddy, I watched Ben for an whole hour. See how responsible I am. I can drive."*
>
> *Everything was about driving. It was driving me crazy. What was on the front of her mind? Driving.*

Our suggestion is, there are certain concepts you, as a business professional should keep at the front of your mind at all times. There are five basic tenets of marketing.

1) Get 'em to **come in**.
2) Get 'em to **try it.**
3) Get 'em to **like it.**
4) Get 'em to **come back**.
5) Get 'em to **endorse you**.

The efficiency, productivity, and profitability of every company in every industry can be evaluated in terms of its ability

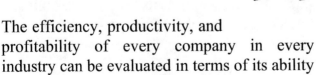

to do these five things. They are as applicable to the obstetrician as they are to General Motors.

Come in. It sounds simple. It is simple. You have got to get the customer in the door. Of course, you already knew that. The real issue is this: is your company doing everything it can to maximize the in-flow of new customers? Is your building accessible and easy to find? Are you spending enough on advertising? Can you acquire more customers through strategic partnerships? Can you afford to expand? Are there demographics you are failing to target? Is there anything about your place of business that would turn people away? Does your company need a Web site? Are there other ways you could be leveraging new informational technologies like the Internet?

Try it. You've got them in the door. They're not going to buy if they don't know what the product is. Bookstores offer free browsing. Ice cream parlors give free samples. Banks will pay you to use their online services. The department store hires ninjas to spray you with perfume or cologne. The best advertising in the world is the smell of baking bread. Are you doing everything you can to introduce your full range of services to the maximum number of customers? Show people what your product is.

Like it. Of course, you want your customer to be satisfied with your service. If the barber cuts your ear off, you're unlikely to go back. But that's not the issue. There are countless companies and professionals that provide perfectly adequate, or even excellent, products and services that are nonetheless doomed to failure. Getting your customers to like it has less to do with the quality of that service than its presentation. Most barbers give a pretty good haircut. Getting your customers to like you means getting them to have a positive emotional experience. You want them to like you and, as much as possible, to enjoy the time they spend with you. Is the receptionist friendly? Is it easy to park? Are there coloring books for the kids? These are the details on which we often base our decisions.

Come back. How do you secure the customer's repeat business? Clearly, the customer's first impression is very important, but it's not the only factor at work. Is your company properly incentivizing repeat business? Should you offer discounts to loyal customers? What lengths will your company go to appease a dissatisfied customer? In the long term, a customer can be worth a lot of money. Treat them that way. Take complaints seriously and do everything within reason to get back into your customers good graces. Can you think of other ways to increase repeat business volume? Your doctor probably tries to schedule your next appointment each time you leave her office. What system do you have in place to re-contact existing customers?

Endorse you. This is as clear as it gets. Never underestimate word-of-mouth. If your customer is in your demographic, so are her friends. How have you incentivized your customer to endorse you? A cash reward? A discount for service? A T-shirt? And if those are not feasible, don't discount asking her to pass the word along. Networking works. If and when we can get our customer to become an "associate marketer" for our business, for US, then we have actualized much of the potential of our marketing department (aka our company).

The tenets of marketing are universal and can be applied to any business in any industry. However, this book can only give you a sketch of how the Psyched on Service Mentality applies to you. Your company and your industry are unique. It's up to you to apply these principles to your own situation. It's up to you find out your strengths and what you can be doing better. Still, if you consistently and scrupulously apply the Psyched on Service Mentality to your business, keep it in the front of your mind, then you will see results. Pragmatically, the issue is learning to question your way of doing business. You want to deroutinize your way of thinking, to find a better way when things are already pretty good. You're in the business of doing it the right way, not of doing business in the old way.

I do suggest that when you're watching Sports Center, or when you're out to dinner with your family, or when you're napping on the couch, you ignore marketing altogether. Other than that, pursue the Psyched on Service Mentality relentlessly. You want to foster in yourself and your employees an attitude of continuous personal improvement. Get everybody on board. Get everybody's input. Then go for it. See everything from the marketing point of view.

In 1982, two marketing colleagues and I invented a marketing medium for small, woman owned and/or minority owned businesses to expose themselves to the US military marketplace for the purpose of securing a portion of those monies set aside for them. We met while consulting with a directory publisher who specialized in marketing to the military families for consumer goods. We advised that the publisher expand their focus on the non-consumer or "business to business" area in- as- much -as the government has money set aside to spend with these types of businesses. We advised that it was a virtually recession proof business. He essentially told us that he was the expert and knew what he was doing... that if we believed in it so much that we should do it ourselves with our own money and "not in his backyard". (Remember the key word: PSYCHOSCLEROSIS) We went for it. In less than 2 years, we had five well-appointed offices servicing the 14 western states and generating millions of dollars in revenue. We literally doubled in size every year for five years.

The business was built on a philosophy that we had to continue to develop our deliverables and subsequent value to our customers ...or die.

So, after publishing the "yellow pages" of ads for the military procurement officers to use and order from, the next year we developed a more comprehensive military marketing plan for the clients. Year after year, we expanded our deliverables to include new and innovative marketing methods for our clients... and they worked. Carpe Diem and keep carping them every Diem.

Chapter 5
DISCONNECT FOUR:

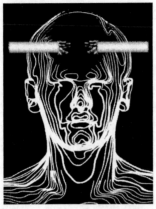

Business has no strategy to recover from mistakes, mishaps, and errors.

When life gives you lemons, make lemonade, not hand grenades. Stupid, crazy, careless, unfortunate things happen. In the ordinary course of business, people are going to make mistakes. It's unavoidable. With the possible exception of Michael Jordan, nobody's perfect at his job. We all have our off days.

The individual employees of a company are like the limbs and appendages of the human body. The actions of all employees of a given corporation reflect at least as much on the company itself as they do on the individual. If they're good, the company benefits. If they're bad, the company suffers the damage. There is no multi-national corporation, no mom-and-pop grocery store, and no law firm in the world that is run with perfect efficiency and without its fair share of errors.

To a certain degree, businesses plan for their mistakes. Just as making mistakes is a natural consequence of any human activity, searching them out is a necessary process of doing business.

The fourth major internal marketing mistake is formulated as follows: The business has no strategy to recover from mistakes, mishaps, and errors. To be more specific, the business has no strategy to correct a bad impression. Front-line employees are not educated how to deal with problem situations. The next chapter will address the issue of how that can be done.

I hired a local pool restoration company to work on my 22 year old in ground swimming pool. These people really talked a good game. They were professional and smooth in every aspect and I felt really confident that they were the ones to do the job. Hence, I engage them. One problem that surfaced was that the subcontractors that they brought in did not subscribe to the same level of professionalism that they did. If fact in one area where they were cleaning out a pail of some sort of acid they threw it on my newly applied sod.

It made this really interesting and yet annoying pattern in my lawn. When I told the company that this had happened and they sent someone out who denied responsibility. They would have earned a lot of good will and what we call associate marketing behavior from me had they gone and spent $8.00 at Home Depot and replaced 2 or 3 pieces of sod. But they didn't. All of their marketing efforts went down the drain with that one silly decision. I guess we need to control not only our own behaviors but also all those who are associated with us and who, in turn, carry our credibility and reputation.

Question:

Who, other than yourself and your direct staff, is carrying your credibility and reputation in the world? Whose actions are affecting your business well being? Is it your courier service? Could it be your Building maintenance service- the ones who are responsible for stocking toilet tissues in your common bathrooms? Whoever they are, it makes sense to determine their quality of deliverables as they are representing YOUR company as much as their own. If their quality standards do not track to yours then THEY could be the weakest link in your marketing efforts and you don't even know it. Hmmmmm.

SYNAPSE FOUR:

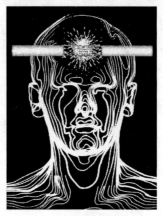

Learning the art of damage control.

Screw up religiously every day, or maybe not.
As a business manager, day to day, the buck
stops with you. It is up to you to educate your
employees as to how to diffuse a problem
situation When the belligerent customer is
yelling for the supervisor, when the worried
mother's child can't be found, when the job is
botched, bungled, and blown to hell, there is a

definite method to address the situation. And

it's something every employee in your organization should know.

First, accept the blame. Basic psychology tells you arguing your point is only going to make the customer even angrier. This is not about your pride. This is not about winning the argument. This is about keeping the customer.

Second, take responsibility. This is neither the time to pass the buck nor to evade the issue. Taking responsibility for the mistake, whatever it is, gives the impression that it is understood there has been a mistake and that you and nobody else is at fault.

Third, empathize. Get the customer on your side by showing him you're on his side. "I know how you must feel. I'd be upset too, if somebody lost my prescription." The goal is changing the situation from one of conflict, to constructive resolution.

Fourth, atone. Make eye contact. Give the customer your name. Let him know you're aware of the problem and you are committed to getting it fixed. In atoning, you are taking the issue out of the customer's hands. He doesn't need to be angry. He doesn't need to make a scene, because you are taking care of it for him.

Finally, follow up. Once again, you have the power to transform a negative experience into a positive one. When the situation is diffused. A simple phone call will do it. Call the customer at home or at work. Let him know how sorry you are for the mistake and assure him it's not typical of your organization. Ask him if he finally got what he needed.

Come to view mistakes not as the death of the relationship, but actually as an opportunity to improve your relationship with the customer. The ordinary course of business is exactly that ordinary. When everything goes as planned, the customer sees an efficient professional. When something goes wrong, the customer should see a caring human being who is doing everything in her power to fix the situation. It should not be a surprising outcome that the mistake cements the customer's loyalty to your organization. After all, they've seen what great people you have working for you!

Grandma used to say, in her lovely British accent, "A lovely china cup that is broken and then glued back together is stronger than before it was broken."

So too is a relationship that was in the process of breaking down but was "glued" back together by your excellent recovery process.

Innovative Service Recovery

Another example of innovative problem solving and service recovery occurred with some colleagues of mine in a company called ResMed Inc. (www.resmed.com), a leader in

Medical Equipment designed to assist in sleep disordered breathing. You might have heard of the medical condition called Sleep Apnea. That is where the sleeping person's air intake is obstructed for a brief time thus causing a 'panic' type response to their body and the resultant harmful effects over time. It is postulated that about 10% of the population suffers from this condition, many of whom are completely in the dark about it. All they know is that they are constantly jabbed by others for snoring; either at home, in movies or theatres, meetings and the like. Carried out into the future, these folk are strong candidates for heart disease and stroke. Why, because in addition to not getting the required amount of deep sleep to 'rebound' properly, they are cycling up and down from sleep to low oxygen saturation and associated body panic and trauma, back into sleep, ad infinitum, ad nauseum, ad vantage harbinger of death. Not a pretty picture, I know, I've

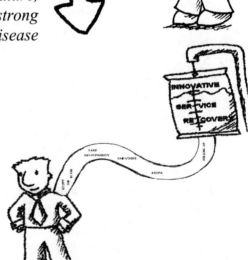

been there. It wasn't until my wife cajoled me to going to a sleep disorder specialist that I could be tested, diagnosed and prescribed the ResMed device to assist me to sleep restoratively through the night. It literally changed my life. I have more energy than I can remember, my vital signs are back where they should be, and my lifestyle has changed to include my thrice a week tennis, seeing movies and plays to their completion, etc. Life is better overall. Not rocket science that if one gets their necessary rests that they will perform more effectively. The big issue was with understanding the symptoms and taking the steps to become diagnosed and treated. I

was interviewed on MDTV, a television program that focuses on current medical issues. The host, internationally renowned Medical Expert, Terry Davidson, M.D., asked me how an educated person, a consultant to the healthcare industry among others, could be living with sleep apnea and not take action to resolve it. Good question but one that needed to be answered with yet another question. I asked Dr. Davidson, how it was that the medical community, one which we spend a large part of our GNP on, could fail us by allowing a patient to go through physicals (which I do yearly), be seen for common sicknesses like virus, sprains, strains and breaks, etc. and never asked on a form or verbally if he snores, so as to query further. I am grateful that my ear, nose and throat Doctor is Dr. Davidson, an accomplished surgeon, the same Doctor who hosts that show and is quite knowledgeable of this disorder. Question: How many of you reading this book snore? (And I can just hear my friends say that they didn't until they read this story!!). Do yourself a favor and go online to learn about sleep apnea. It's killer information.

Another Example of Service Recovery

ResMed, mentioned earlier, has a great example of service recovery through innovation. Perhaps that is partly why they are in the Fortune Small Business 100 list. Here's the situation and how they responded.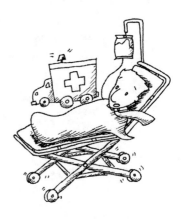

Challenges occurred when customer service representatives would open a distributor account to sell a sleep-breathing device only to experience a time glitch in delivery due to the credit check process. In some cases, the distributor would take the path of least resistance and simply sell that patient a different brand of equipment, one that was perhaps better known, already established with their credit department- even if it was not as good. Clearly, this minimized the value to the distributor, the patient and most certainly ResMed as the manufacturer. The solution was, again, a re-combination of existing elements. They created customer support teams consisting of Sales Representatives as well as Credit Department Representatives. In fact, they physically moved these people together so that they could facilitate answers in as close to real time as possible. If the answer is not immediately available, a personal representative will do the legwork and get back to the customer the same day, most often within the hour. Any credit or payment issues are handled while the customer is on the telephone for ease of shipment. Bottom line, it works.

You Control Your Life!
Don't You?

It might not feel like it on Monday morning, but you control your destiny every day you go to work. Under the press of our financial obligations and our personal commitments, it's easy to lose sight of that autonomy.

It bears consideration that your company may or may not be right for you. The next two chapters will discuss the importance of work culture and how to find the culture right for you.

Regaining your sense of control is critical to improving your working life. Furthermore, it underpins every concept this book is illustrating. A philosophy of change is meaningless without a firm belief that change is not only possible, but immediately available. Pro-active change depends on your belief that your environment is under your control.

That belief is a powerful tool. Believe it. You can do what you want. You'll probably never fill the swimming pool with champagne; you'll probably never remodel Graceland for your great aunt Tina. But who wants to? You can make your life what you want it to be. (And maybe you can get Tina a ticket to Memphis.)

With the possible exception of Tiger Woods, almost everybody has a few things he'd like to change about his job. Problem: My morning commute takes an hour in traffic.

> **Solution:** Go in early. Get the busy work done before the traffic hits.

Or maybe that's not the solution for you. The point is, most often a problem has a workable solution. There are things you can do to make your life better.

> **Problem:** I could do more. My supervisor gives me no responsibility.

> **Solution One:** Ask for more responsibility.
>> or
> **Solution Two:** Take the initiative. Do something that shows you deserve the responsibility. Graph the figures you think she ought to see.
>> or
> **Solution Three:** Show someone else you've got what it takes. Prepare your figures and speak up in the meeting. Get noticed!

It may not work. If it doesn't, chances are, there's something wrong with the company and it's time to play that ace up your sleeve. There are better places for a change-oriented pro-active professional like you.

But there's a good chance that it will work. And if it does, you've done yourself an enormous favor. Remake your job into what you want it to be. Your job can be more than a business casual fashion show and a paycheck twice a month. If you make your work exciting, it can be a lasting source of fulfillment to you.

Remember 'The Law of Control': We feel good about ourselves to the extent we are in control of our lives

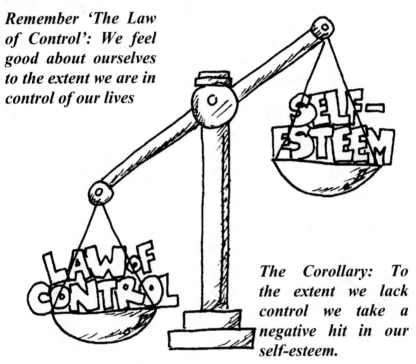

The Corollary: To the extent we lack control we take a negative hit in our self-esteem.

Your self-esteem suffers when you're not calling the important shots in your life. Get involved! You're not being selfish by asking for what you want. You're not being pushy either. You're asking to get in the game. The more you can involve yourself in the decision-making processes of your company, the better you'll feel about yourself and the more valuable you'll be to your employers.

That's something any reasonable boss will understand. If you find yourself shut out of the process, then you need to reexamine the kind of corporate culture that doesn't want your input and decide if it's the place for you.

It's your call. Control what you can. Place your hands squarely on the steering wheel of the direction of your life and go joy riding with that attitude. To quote that great philosopher, Kenneth Rogers, "you've got to know when to holdem' know when to foldem'."

Culture Counts

How to make your job work for you

This book has repeatedly emphasized the importance of how you work and where you work. There's a good reason for that. The working environment you choose is critical for every aspect of your success. Your job security depends on the ability of your company to innovate, adapt, and survive in a mercenary economy. Your own ability to contribute and to take an active role in company life is limited by the culture fostered by the organization.

This book has repeatedly raised the issue that your current company may not be the culture for you. Not because quitting is option one, but because knowing it's an option is the first step towards a better working life.

It's simple negotiating strategy: you must always come to the table knowing you can walk away. I've read that referred to as the BATNA, the Best Alternative To A Negotiated Agreement. That knowledge is the beginning of a revolution in your attitude towards working. That knowledge gives you permission to try outrageous things, like innovating, like striving for success, like trying to make a difference. Because if you try and it doesn't work, you'll know you're not stuck.

How do you know if your company's the right culture for you?

Is it professional? Or does Becky or Bubba in marketing spend all day gossiping on the phone? Your colleagues should share your sense of purpose. Everyone should recognize there's work to be done and that some behaviors are inappropriate for the workplace. You don't want to work in a Styrofoam beehive, but this is business and some sense of efficiency is called for. You want to be a class act. And you want to work for one.

Is it caring? Revenues are the life's blood of business, but customer service is its heart. How much heart does your company have? Caring sells itself. Attitude matters. Is there an elevator up to your office and a wheelbarrow out? There shouldn't be. In the long run, taking care of the customer is the best way to take care of the bottom line.

Is there a climate of mutual respect? Do you care what your coworkers think? Do they care what you think? Are you getting your work done in spite of them or with their help? The ideal work environment is collegial. You're all colleagues. You work together, so work together. Everyone around you should be a resource and you should make yourself available to your colleagues. The more valuable each team member feels, the more he's going to want to help the team.

Is it positive? The benefits of a positive work culture cannot be overstressed. Do the people in your office like each other? It's an important question. If people don't like each other, how likely are they to want to help each other? Management must do everything it can to foster a positive working environment. Gossip is cancerous in the workplace. It breeds distrust and inefficiency. In its worst form, it leads to an "us versus them" dynamic between management and employees, doing incalculable harm inside the organization and to the company's public image. Conversely, positivity breeds efficiency, unity, and customer enthusiasm. So it's worth asking the question: what is your company doing to bring people together?

Is it fun? Work can be fun. And if you're having fun, if you enjoy what you do, you're going to do it better. It's that simple. Sure, it's not Mardi Gras in the skyscrapers and business parks of America, but a company on the rise will invest itself in a positive work environment and the happiness of its workers. It's the smart move. The best people find the best jobs and the best companies know it.

A company that conducts itself in a professional manner, that cares about the customer, that fosters a climate of positivity and mutual respect, that wants its employees to get the most out of working is a winner. And a company that doesn't is not. If that's what you've got, make the most of it. If that's what you want, go get it!

Now you know the culture you're looking for. Learn to market yourself with that culture in mind. Be pro-active. Invest in yourself. Take control of your job. And find the company for you. Apply the Psyched on Service Mentality to everything you do.

One asset of such a company is that they have a Mission Statement that is actually functional, in use and alive. Here's a great example of **Culture in action:**

One of our clients is a 3 billion dollar mortgage lender and servicer of loans. Mountain States Mortgage Centers' Founder and CEO, J.R. Green, took our "mission statement" delivery system very, very much to heart. In fact at every one of their major meetings be it a management meeting or an entire company wide meeting, they always start with someone reading the mission statement. And they had fun with it. I remember distinctly being invited to a meeting with the entire company present. A manager approached the front of the room, wearing a Blues Brother's style outfit, holding a saxophone and started the meeting by playing the saxophone then putting it down for a second and in a beatnik tone stated,

"Mission statement, oh yeah." He then squeaked out some notes and then read another line of the mission statement. This went on until everyone was completely hysterical. And by the way, over 80% of the people there are now able to recite the mission statement word for word at any given point. They have fun with it and they recognize that the mission statement is a very, very integral part of their work environment. It's not just a statement on the wall. It's something that they live and work by. Their productivity per employee is heads and shoulders over their industry standard and they have earned a profit in every quarter of their 18 years in business. How cool is that?

Chapter 6
DISCONNECT FIVE:

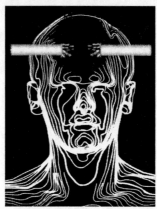

Front-line employees are not taught the communication skills they need to be effective.

It's not what you say, but how you say it.

The last of the major internal marketing mistakes is relatively straightforward and is easy to formulate. Front-line employees are not taught the communication skills they need to be effective. Just as every one of us has recently joined the marketing department, we have also switched industries. The preponderant component of every industry is communication. We are all in communications. A full understanding of the Psyched on Service Mentality requires an appreciation for the value of communication. Yet, the communication skills that are so vital to success in every industry are often neglected. Years ago, a study was conducted by Dr. Mehrabian at UCLA. The purpose of the study was to analyze communication and its components. Those components were: the verbal, which are the words we speak; the vocal, which is the tone of voice we use when speaking; and the visual, which is body language or the posture we take while speaking. What Dr. Mehrabian found was remarkable.

On a percentile basis, he attributed 93% of all communication to nonverbal signals. 38% he attributed to tone of voice and 55% to our body language. Think about that. Only 7% of our communication is verbal.

In part, we can summarize Dr. Mehrabian's study by an old standby: "It's not what you say, but how you say it."

Among other mistakes prompted by their lack of communication skills, employees are led to believe that going through the motions is good enough. Well, it turns out they're dead wrong.

When you're unhappy, when you're frustrated, when you let it show that you're unhappy and frustrated and that the cat poked its claws in the waterbed that morning, the customers know it. My observation is that customers are like puppies and children. They know when you are incongruent.

Great Example of how this works. How many of us have sung our children to sleep with that old standard, "Rock-a-bye Baby"? You remember, *"Rock-a-bye Baby, on a treetop. When the wind blows the cradle will rock. When the bow breaks the cradle will fall, and down will come baby, cradle and all."*

Think about it, we tell our beautiful child that they will hang from a tree, the wind will come and blow them out of the tree, that their cradle will come crashing down to the ground and, oh bye the way, have sweet dreams sweetheart! What do they do? They ooh and ahh and gurgle and enjoy your loving voice... no matter what you say. You could inject words into the melody like, "Attila the Hun will baby-sit you tonight, pull off your head and suck out your guts" and the baby is totally cool with it – as long as your other communication cues from your tone, your eyes, your facial expression are warm and loving.

In Burt Decker's book, <u>You've Got To Be Believed To Be Heard,</u> he makes the point that our eyes scan the communicators' face and appearance immediately and in an instant we make decisions as to whether we like or trust that person or not. Decker cites some great studies to make the point. Relevant to this chapter is his observation that we often listen with our eyes, we take in the information at an unconscious level and make decisions at that level as to whether we are dealing with friend or foe (my words).

Another great example of that comes from some training that my brother Howie Corbin presented at his tele-sales company, my first summer sales job in 1974. They sold industrial supplies via the telephone- a customer convenience that pre-dated the internet. He taught us that it was only natural and instinctive for the prospect to object to the sale until they had some sense of our legitimacy. He taught us to say, in response to any objection, the following, DAIN SAIN ANYWAY, AND IM SURE YOU'D AGREE!

What? You want me to say, DAIN SAIN ANYWAY, AND IM SURE YOU'D AGREE?

What language is that? I asked, are you nuts?

We tried it. It worked. The purchasing agents responded with, "that's a good point" or "I see what you mean."

I DIDN'T SAY ANYTHING... yet they agreed. That proved to me then and now that Dr. Mehrabian was spot on. It is not what you say; it's how you say it that makes all the difference. In all of my communications I actively seek to be aware of that. Thanks Howie.

Listen to your dog

I can recall years ago living in Princeton, N.J. with some really interesting and bright roommates. My dog loved everyone but Jimbo. Every time Jimbo came near, my dog Arnold would growl. For everyone else Arnold had nothing but love. Some months later it became apparent that Jimbo was not who he purported to be. He was not exactly the friend that we thought him to be... and my dog knew it before us. Can't fool some animals. It has been my experience that customers, kids and canines are in the category of reading people carefully & clearly at all sensory levels.. I've heard it said that "everyone knows everything." Why even try to BS? Go figure.

The next chapter will help the business manager provide his employees with some of the tools necessary for effective communication. (Even if YOU are the only employee in You, Inc.)

SYNAPSE FIVE (the last one!):

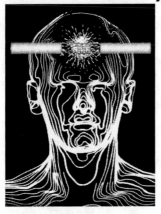

Applying the science of interpersonal communication.

No doubt that you realize that The Psyched on Service Mentality is an attitude about success. In each of the five internal marketing solutions, this book has stressed the necessity of approaching problems from a pro-active appearance-oriented frame of thought.

To varying degrees, every employee of every organization is on public display. As the new head of the marketing department, the business manager must do everything possible to enforce a standard of excellence. Appearance is everything.

A slumping receptionist isn't wishing you all that happy a day, no matter how cheerful her voice. If you act like you don't want to be at work, everyone will know it. It's that simple. It's a recurrent problem: Front-line employees are not taught the communication skills they need to be effective.

The Psyched on Service Mentality means using everything, you've got to make a good impression. Communication is the life's blood of almost every human endeavor, especially in our professional life. Without the tools to communicate effectively, the front-line employee, the technician, the computer consultant, the receptionist, the nurse, the optician, the kindergarten teacher is hamstrung.

What amazes me is how simple the communication techniques are to teach, and understand. That's not to say that they're obvious. We simply don't teach them enough. After this brief example, we will share some of these specific strategies for you to use immediately.

In terms of communication, people can be classified as visual auditory or kinesthetic processors. Visual processors, as the name implies, process information primarily through seeing. Auditory processors process information primarily through hearing. Kinesthetic processors process information primarily through touching.

Sounds simple, is simple. Nevertheless, this little lesson in neurolinguistics can go a long way towards teaching the front-line professional how to establish a rapport with the customer.

It has been established experimentally that the preferred language of visual processors has an astonishingly visual bias. "I **see** what you're saying." An auditory processor might say, "I **hear** you." Alternatively, a kinesthetic processor might say, "I think I've got a good **grasp** on that."

The first step of establishing a rapport is this: speak the language of the person you're talking to. If you are talking to an auditory processor who is asking, "Do you **hear** what I'm saying?" do not respond with, "Yeah, I see your point." Subconsciously, there's a clash. Instead, tell him, "**Loud and clear**." You're aiming at matching the customer's language and not just, in terms of what kind of processor you're speaking to. If the customer is speaking fast, speak fast. If the customer is freewheeling gregarious, let yourself be loose. Professional but loose. If the customer is more reserved, then be friendly but reserved. If the customer leans in towards you, lean in. If the customer whispers, whisper. It's simple, but it's powerful.

Jewboys and Indians

Bridging the gap in communication and rapport is exemplified in my relationship with my Native American clients and friends, of which I count many in my life.

Fact is the Native Americans have been screwed over by our wonderful country from their earliest relations together. If you have seen the condition of life on some of the earliest established reservations then you wouldn't dare take me to task on that statement. The perpetuation of poverty, drug and alcohol abuse and the like continued (and in some areas I suspect continues) on some of these Reservations until we co-developed Indian owned and operated enterprises including Indian Gaming Centers. We were fortunate enough to work with some of these California Nations early on, while they were still not compacted or "blessed" by the California Government. All involved, including myself and other vendors, advisors and associates were somewhat at risk. Still, though, we were not completely trusted white men and women. The Indians had too many experiences built up to be foolish enough to easily trust the "white man" and who could blame them?

In searching for common ground between these folk and myself, I realized some strong similarities between their Tribes and mine. What follows is totally true. Here's how I articulated it:

It was common to start a meeting with Indians with introductions as to who you were, where you were from, what tribe, etc. When it came to be my turn I responded as follows:

"I am David Corbin. I am from a tribe that has been around a bit longer than just about all of yours. It has been dumped on longer than most of yours. It is the Tribe of Jews." (Usually I would draw applause, smiles and acknowledgement as a member of yet another tribe.). I would go on to say, "However, thanks to my forefathers, I am here today, reasonably well educated, obviously well fed (overweight sic) and thankfully, clothed. My early relatives united early on, worked their butts off in untenable conditions, long hours, differing in culture and language, and rather than spending their money frivolously, they invested in education and learning for themselves and their family. They held sacred their traditions and the ways of their people, their Tribe. Their sacrifices have gifted me even today."

That communication bridge came from my head and my heart. It stands today as my belief system and the foundation of my relationship with many Native Tribal Leaders throughout the US. I think back to times when I had no articulation of that and would possibly have been regarded as another white man who was primarily interested in personal gain and potentially in the continued exploitation of Indians.

Rapport gives you a measure of control. The more the customer (internal or external) feels connected to you, the more he wants to keep up the rapport. It's not hypnotism but it is a more persuasive tool than many people realize. Keep in mind that the God Only Knows (GOK) factor of doing business is a powerful motivator... and however your rapport is established, GOK, it is a bond worth maintaining.

The Unit of Conviction method of communicating:

In this over-communicated society in which we find ourselves, it is no surprise that most people we meet are jaded, calloused and generally skeptical. After all, let's face it; we are confronted-shall I say bombarded- with over 5,000 commercial messages per day. How then do we capture attention of our *communication prospect*, differentiate ourselves from the herd of marketers, and be heard in such a way that we do not invoke that oppositional reflex in which they say, think, or feel, "so what", "yeah right" or "gimme a break, willya?"

Here's how it works:

'You can be sure we provide the highest quality stereo equipment at the lowest prices.'

The claim is followed by a **supporting fact**.

'Stereophile magazine ranked us the number one discount hi-fi dealer in Southern California.'

The claim and the fact are joined by the word "**because**."

'You can be sure we provide the highest quality stereo equipment at the lowest prices, **because** Stereophile magazine ranked us the number one discount hi-fi

dealer in Southern California.

This is followed by a phrase to the effect **"which means to you**."

'You can be sure we provide the highest quality stereo equipment at the lowest prices, because Stereophile magazine ranked us the number one discount hi-fi dealer in Southern California which means to you a good night's sleep knowing you got the best deal possible.'

In turn, this statement is followed by an explanation.

The reason I say this is our customers seem to appreciate knowing our credentials.

While the formula may seem a little contrived, the unit of conviction forces the speaker into a persuasive mode of speech, considers the potential skepticism, avoids the oppositional reflex button and thus disarms the listener's ability to shrug him off. The claim is immediately substantiated by a fact. The significance of the claim and fact to the listener are established by showing the immediate benefit to the listener and explaining the motive for the comment.

Have you ever heard or read a Unit of Conviction like statement? Bet you did! There's one on the fourth paragraph of this book's Introduction. Check it out.

The benefits of such techniques to any professional are enormous and are ample material for a whole series of books. For our purposes here, we have only meant to show by these techniques that the business manager can, in addressing the deficient communication skills of his front-line employees, lead his company to a more effective way of doing business.

A Unit of Conviction Example

In working with a group of employees at the Veterans Administration Medical Center, we found that there was a problem with the enormity of the parking lot and the distance that the infirmed patient needed to walk from their car to the front door. Well the maintenance people came up with an idea. They posed, "Why don't we get some sort of golf carts and drive the patients from their car to the front door?" They proposed it to the management. Of course the management said, "No, can't be done." "Why?" " We're not budgeted for it." Well this team decided to go back to the drawing board and considered, "Well, why can't we get them donated by some of the local car companies who would then put advertising on the side and donate the carts for free. They proposed it to the management whose job it seemed to be to shoot it down which indeed they did in saying that, "We don't have the staff. Would you and your people be willing to go further?" Well these people certainly were. And they did. They recognized that there are a number of Veteran service groups, The Foreign Wars Veterans, The Jewish War Veterans, The Disabled Veterans that were willing to drive the carts on a no fee basis and be able to take the people from the car to the front door. They brought it to the management and the management at this point realized that there were possibilities here and they moved forward. One thing that did beyond that is that they also educated each driver on a "Units of Conviction", a unique way of communicating the capabilities of the hospital in meaningful terms to the patient while on that short ride. And I gotta tell you that the customer rating in service index when they did the cart went up by 65%. When they included "Units Of Conviction" to be communicated by these volunteer staff from point A to the front door the ratings went up another 30%. Clearly, they almost doubled the patient satisfaction index with the innovated suggestions of their maintenance staff at little or no additional cost. Well done.

Further, if the path outlined in this book were followed to the end, the benefits, not only to the company but also to every single employee of the company, would be incalculably great.

If you as a business manager have the courage to face the challenges your company's failings offer, if you make the determination to instill the Psyched on Service Mentality in each and every one of your employees, you will have made heroic strides on their behalf. You will have a team full of winners. And winners win.

A case study - Communicating to Save Lives

Have you ever been to the Doctor's office, fully intending to mention something relevant to your current state of health or unhealth, only to forget it? Seems we remember it only when we are back in our car on our way home. Can you relate? Fact is, many; many people have shared this experience with us. Something happens that we get caught up in the medical exam and visit experience. This disconnect in communication is potentially critical There is some evidence that our forgetfulness is associated with fear and anxiety stemming from the medical visit. In fact, Doctors have suspected that the many patients with high blood pressure -- or hypertension -- who don't seem to be improving under treatment may have what is often called **white coat hypertension**. That means that the stress of being in the doctor's office and having their blood pressure measured may make their blood pressure go up temporarily. The effect is not limited to blood chemistry and physiology. There are psychological effects too. As mentioned above, we can easily forget to mention some or many of the things we had fully intended to mention.

The conundrum can be significant. If, for example, we forget to mention to our Doctor that we are on a certain medication or that we are allergic to yet another then there could be a drastically negative implication.

Too many times, we hear of missed diagnoses. Too many times, we hear of patients going into a Doctor's office with challenges that are totally and completely un-addressed. That is why my business partner and I invented the StatusView touch screen patient interview system. The patient would answer questions that were designed to facilitate or prompt their keeping these issues at front of mind. Hence, fewer issues go un-addressed. This was an innovation that used existing components, standard computer monitors, touch screen overlay, patient surveys and medical intake forms and blended them in a unique manner with which we were honored with the Innovation of the Year by Bank of America. Simple, easy and it worked for all parties, the Doctors, their Staff, the Patient and certainly my company and team.

Communication counts

There's a concept called Pre-Framing where you actually lead the thoughts and behaviors of others by essentially telling them what they will think and feel in the future.

Future Pacing – A great communication and persuasion tool.

A good example rests in a situation that one of my clients found themselves in. They are in the business of selling home flooring. You know, carpeting, tile, linoleum etc. They had contracts with homebuilders who would then give the homebuyer an allowance to be spent with my client. My client would then show them the flooring that was standard for the home, discuss with them lifestyle issues, and then where applicable the homebuyer might move from carpeting to hard surfaces such as tile, wood, or linoleum. An example would be if they eat while watching TV, they might want to get a hard surface that might clean up easier. However, they were also in the business of selling window treatments, shades, blinds, and alike. Unfortunately, however, by the time the trained designer would complete the flooring needs evaluation and selection the customer would have been there over an hour. Then the designer would start discussing the window treatment needs and the homebuyer would psychologically check out and not be interested in that part of my client's offerings. Our solution was not very complicated but it really, really worked.

Here it is: We suggested that the designer touch the customer's hand at a point where the customer was really excited about a selection or a recommendation made by the designer. Coupled with touching their hand, we had the designer say, "Wait until we get to the window treatment or the window covering of today's meeting. You're really gonna love it." This future paced the homebuyer into knowing that there is a window treatment discussion for today's meeting. This way when they get to the window treatment discussion it's not a surprise.

Here's a real example of its effectiveness. One day a woman came in with her young daughter to select the flooring. The designer did exactly what she was trained to do She touch the customer's hand and mention the window covering at the appropriate time. Well as it happened the little girl, some 20 minutes into their meeting got sick and threw up all over the carpeting samples. The designer excused herself to get paper towels (and told me that she too almost threw up) and came back and with the mother was cleaning up. The only thing the mother said was, "Oh I am so sorry, and we didn't even get to the window treatments yet. Can we clean her up and do that now?"

Do you see the power of future pacing? Remember it happens best when it is linked or associated with something very, very positive. By the way, the homebuyer did reschedule and the designer not only got the flooring sale with a significant amount of upgrades but also sold and covered every window in their new home. It worked.

Idea:

How can you use this powerful communication technique to benefit your goals and the goals of your team.

Chapter 7
CREATING LEGENDS

By completing the circuit

You are only as good as your customers think you are. That's a lesson most business managers learn quickly on their own. This book has discussed in other chapters the necessity for any business of upholding the reputation and credibility of the company name. Impression management is part of every employee's job description. From the receptionist to the assistant junior part-time copyboy right on up to the business manager, part of everybody's job is giving the customer a Positive Emotional Experience. If it were possible, I would skip printing those three words here and include a miniature neon sign instead.

The tasks assigned to every job are different. The difficulties that come with every position are different. The compensation and authority that go with every title are different. But we can democratize business this much: it is everybody's job to make the customer feel good about our company. If the business manager is any different in this regard, it is only in that she must hold everybody accountable for the new standards she is

127

setting for the company. She must uphold the reputation and credibility of the company and make sure that everyone else does too.

Is that all there is to it? Not by a long shot. Quality service is a beginning, but it's not the whole story. It is necessary to success, but not sufficient. The business manager who aims at not screwing up has blown it already.

Economics as we know it assumes competition at the fiercest level. And general wisdom leads us to believe that the competition is for money. On the most superficial level, we know this to be true. The Psyched on Service Mentality teaches us that success begins with maintaining a positive relationship with the customer. The bottom line, revenues, profits, money, Porsches, Rolexes, and fishing trips to Cabo are the fruit of those relationships. As the gambler once said, you can sheer a sheep a dozen times, but you can only skin him once. Less cynically, while we've got to keep an eye on the bottom line -- we all know that-- the best way to serve ourselves is to serve the customer.

For a moment, then, let's reconceive of the competition in marketing terms. Instead of a competition for dollars, we have a competition for customers. That reconception should do nothing to soften our idea of how fierce that competition can be. If anything, competing for customers is a far tougher and dirtier fight. If you have your doubts, how many times has

MCI or AT&T called your house this year? How many times this month has, a credit card company sent you convenience checks promising a low-rate balance transfer? How many times today have you seen an ad promising to do it better, faster, cheaper than whoever's doing it now? They aren't just looking for a couple of bucks. They are gunning for your business. They want you for life.

In a world of extreme competition, we must radically alter our perception of how we influence the behavior of customers. We cannot afford to simply, go through the motions.

Chances are, you've got competitors. Chances are, they're pretty good at what they do. It is no longer good enough to make an adequate impression. It is no longer good enough not to screw up.

Your company is not going to give good service. Your company is going to give legendary service. How do we do that? How do we give service so good, how do we create a reputation so bulletproof, that we are irreplaceable? How do we convince our customers that nobody can do the job we can? The short answer is: by doing the things nobody else will.

We must create our own legends. Legends of extraordinary service. To get specific, a legend is a story that is passed down and believed to be true. Only you can determine what legends your company will create. Eighty-year-old Mrs. Jenkins will remember you helping her sort her pills for the week to come. The young mother will remember you giving her fidgety toddler some crayons to pass the time. The family of five will remember getting a ride home in their auto mechanic's mini-van. And, more importantly, they will tell everyone they know about it.

To give you an idea of what I mean, I am going to give you a couple of real-life examples. All are true stories. All are legends of extraordinary service.

Legend One: *Thinking on your feet.*

A hospital cafeteria worker's primary job, which he did well, was to heat up trays of food

before they were sent out to patients and hospital staff. In a typical day, the cafeteria served about nine thousand trays of food. Moreover, this particular worker, a Young immigrant named Jaime, was responsible for a large percentage of the trays. One particular tray was sent back by a third-floor patient who complained that the food arrived cold. Jaime reheated the food and sent it back upstairs. Well, the food came back down again. Jaime patiently realized there was a sick person on the receiving end of the food assembly line and one probably not too satisfied with the hospital cafeteria. Jaime took the opportunity. He reheated the tray, found a rose to add to the tray, and sent it upstairs with a handwritten note that read, in broken English: "Sorry food cold. Hope this better."

While we never determined whether the food was subsequently delivered hot. We did find out that Jaime created a Legend. Just about everybody on that floor heard about Jaime's act of creative care.

Legend Two: *Empowered employees take action.*

A man walked into the Nordstrom's in Anchorage, Alaska, upset that the tires on his car were wearing badly. He approached a salesperson, made his complaint, stated he'd paid $100 per tire, and asked for his money back. The salesperson gave his name, said, "Yes sir, let me speak to my manager please," and went back to talk to his manager. Now he got to the back room, told the manager the customer's complaint, told the manager the customer's demands, reminded the manager that Nordstrom's doesn't sell tires, and do you know what that manager said? He said, "Give him his money back." And that's what the salesperson did. He went out and refunded the customer his $400, for tires, the customer certainly didn't purchase at Nordstrom's.

Now that's a true story. What does it mean? Am I asking you to give out $400 to anyone who asks for it? Of course not. But in giving the man his money back, the manager created a true legend of extraordinary service. I told this story in a seminar and a full ten percent of the seminar had heard it before. From a marketing point of view, imagine the impact of that $400 gesture if ten percent of the population, or even one percent, of the population has heard that story. 2.5 million people's good opinion of Nordstrom's is worth a lot more than $400. Immeasurably more! Now would the same tactic work for you? Possibly not. But it's up to you to recognize the opportunities you do have, however unusual, however counterintuitive they may seem.

Legend Three *Adapting fast.*
David Pemberton, one of the brightest training consultants in the nation, shared this Legend with me. Apparently, he was doing a training workshop with a small group of 50 managers in Denver. The very engaged group was very disappointed when the lights went out, literally. The electricity was down and no one knew how long he or she would have to suspend his or her class. Happily enough, one of the participants had arrived that day on a motorcycle. The motorcyclist suggested, because they were on the ground floor and

adjacent to the parking lot, that he maneuver the bike inside the room and point the light in such a way that they could continue the program. They did, and it worked! Now that's a testimony to two major points: Pemberton is an engaging workshop leader... and this group was resourceful as all get out. I can assure you that there are people out there sharing the legend about their motorcycle-illuminated training.

Legend Four *Persistence Rules!*
Kevin Thornton, founder of KP Gaming, colleague and friend relates this fine example of Legendary Service.

Even though I was prospecting and hopeful to get this 'soon to open' Indian Casino's business, they awarded their business to a competitor much larger than my business. That competitor, however, was rather complacent with this small Indian Casino. With just three days before their grand opening, they were informed that their gaming tables were not going to be ready. That's when they called me. I guess I could have told them to buzz off but they were in need and I could certainly always use the business. In less than 3 days of working day and night, we produced their custom card tables... much of it right there in their parking lot! We really went for it, we pulled it off and they were, needless to say, very appreciative. Throughout the last 5 years or so, we became their vendor of choice when it came to gaming tables and stools. Of course, we had to perform and be competitive but that extra effort really solidified our relationship.

Now, they are expanding big time. They have teamed up with Donald Trump and his group and are opening a huge destination resort casino venue. Trump's people always use their own vendor for tables and chairs, they call the shots and that's that. Well, not with this Indian Casino. They TOLD the Trump people that they were buying their tables and stools from me and that was that. Bottom line, I got the business. Now the large casino suppliers are wondering just who this medium sized manufacturer and distributor in Riverside California is and how they "trumped" all of the other Trump suppliers. It's sort of created what David refers to as a Service Legend. When we perform for this project, we anticipate that our business will take a quantum leap into those strata of the market. And all stemmed from going the extra mile for this small band of Indians when others would not. Not rocket science, just good sound business principles.

Legends like these add to a business' reputation in a way that cannot be bought with advertising dollars. What can you do to create legends of your own? It's a question only you can answer. Get inspired! Everybody has to get involved. This is your company's chance to rise above the rest, to thrive when others merely survive. If you do make the investment in enlisting your staff, if you do strive to create your own legends of extraordinary service, you'll have taken the first major stride towards a culture of success and long-term customer loyalty.

Funny how certain things leave an impression in your mind and others, well, they simply pass by our conscious awareness. I can vividly remember attending a management-training workshop at The Woodlands Texas entitled, Models for Management. It was developed by Dr. Jay Hall, a brilliant author and consultant in the field of Manager Development. If you get the chance to read his book, <u>The Competence Connection,</u> do so as it will give you a succinct overview of Management theory from early on to present.

Their workshop was superb. Well developed, well presented and attended by some very sharp managers who were equally impressed. At one point in the seminar, they showed a film, Twelve Angry Men. Perhaps you've seen it. They cleverly related it to the process of gaining consensus. As clever as it was, using the movie and blending it into the application exercise, what most people talked about after the process was the following: during the film they cooked and handed out little bags of popcorn! Not caviar, not Lobster Newberg, just good old popcorn and THAT'S what people remembered before anything else. Not that we want to obscure the major point of the seminar, but we do want to give the attendee that positive emotional experience... and the popcorn was a great catalyst to that. Well-done Dr. Hall!

Another great example of creating a positive impression comes from my son's Dentist. After the visit, later that evening, he personally phones and asks how my son is feeling. No great shakes but it sure creates an impression in our family that he is a caring health provider. While one of my best friends is a local Dentist and I would prefer to have the whole family go to the same Dentist for convenience, there is no way that anyone can pry my son away from his existing Dentist. And the bond was formed and is maintained by a simple 2 minute phone call or voice message on the voicemail. Small investment for large payoff, wouldn't you agree?

PSYCHED ON SERVICE
Peripheral Vision

Have you ever noticed that you never see a Subaru until your neighbor purchases one? Also, isn't it amazing that whenever I need to buy tires for my car that the local newspaper runs full-page tire ads...just for me?

It happens every day... or does it. Clearly, the difference lies with my perceptions and nothing else. It is a function of the mental filters that we have controlling our awareness.

Reticular Activator System: a group of cells at the base of our skull that filters out information or allows certain information into our conscious minds. Once I allow the Subaru into my Reticular Activator System then I will notice them regularly.

My challenge to you is to open your Reticular Activator System for service Legends. Where can YOU create a service Legend? Chances are that you don't know right now. Or maybe you do. I can assure you, though, that when you program your mind to look for these opportunities, you will definitely find them. Where is it written, "seek and ye shall find?" Oh, that's right.

Creating Legends is a habit. Be careful. You might just gain a reputation for yourself and your business that is superb. You might just earn that job security that you seek. Also, you might achieve a level of job satisfaction that is off the charts. As Grandma often said, "it should only be so."

THE PROMISED LAND: The Psyched on Service Culture

Deserve Your Success

In beginning this book, I wrote that the Unfailing Step-By-Step Guide to Professional Success and Personal Perfection is not currently available in stores. There's a good reason for that. Nobody knows what it takes for you to succeed. The challenges of managing your business and of fulfilling your professional potential are unique.

Now I want to add a second volume to the Imaginary Library of Nonexistent Books. To my knowledge, there has never been a book called How to Make Six Figures by Being a Lazy Idiot.

The secret of success is not a secret. Success requires dedication. It requires intelligence. It requires teamwork. It requires consistency. Success requires work.

I know my audience. Anybody taking the time to read this book has already made the commitment to succeed. By any measuring stick, you're a success already.

But there is no finish line in business. The Psyched on Service Mentality is not a road map to success. The Psyched on Service

Mentality is a course in defensive driving. The question is not how do I succeed, but how do I keep my success, how do I keep on improving as a business manager?

Ultimately, the Psyched on Service Mentality is an attitude towards success. This book is about acquiring a mindset that perpetuates our success. This book is about enrolling an entire business in a culture that perpetuates its success. Along the way, I have tried to give some practical suggestions for implementing it in your own life and in the lives of your employees. But it's the attitude that matters!

What is that attitude? It's a desire for continuous personal improvement, an openness to the idea that there is always something we can do to better address our customer's needs. It's a realization that every interaction with the customer is an opportunity to market ourselves to that customer. It's a drive to transform our way of doing business, to revolutionize every employee's way of thinking about doing business. It's the knowledge that your company is capable of being better than good. You can be the best. You are capable of legendary feats of extraordinary service.

I mentioned Andy Gove's Book <u>entitled</u> <u>Only The Paranoid Survive</u> as you may recall. One of my early mentors offered another spin on that topic. He explained *that the Paranoid believe that the world is conspiring to HURT them.*

He further offered that it would best serve us all to become the Inverse Paranoid – one who believes that the world is conspiring to HELP them. Sounded good then so I tried that attitude on for size and I can tell you now, some 15 years later, that it has been a very powerful catalyst for positive change in my life. It goes back to the adage,
Seek and ye shall find." It is the "fundamental principle in my change management programs.
Argue that the change is great even when you don't believe that it is. Open your mind to possibilities. Anticipate the best, expect the best and accept the best. What if the world was indeed conspiring to help you? Might you look closer for the positive attributes of either that person, or that change initiative or whatever comes down the line?

I know the benefits of the Psyched on Service Mentality. I've seen it work! Many years of consulting with organizations such as The Veterans Administration, Kaiser Permanente, Motorola, Countrywide Mortgage and others as well as masterminding with other

Consultants have helped formulate these learnings. The principles embodied in this book are at work in the most successful companies in the country. I believe that they will work for you as well.

By engaging your employees in the Psyched on Service Mentality, by showing them their role in the overall marketing strategy of your organization, you enroll them in a team effort. You make them a part of the decision-making process and, more importantly, you give them a feeling of decision-making responsibility or at least the decision influencing responsibility toward the company's success. If you show your team how the Psyched On Service Mentality leads to their personal job security, if you preach the gospel of continuous personal improvement, if you foster a positive and collegial business culture, you're simply not going to believe your eyes.

Dr. Jay Hall, mentioned earlier, shared with me that there is an important triangle at work in most flourishing organizations. At the three points of the triangle, we find these words: Collaboration, Creativity and Commitment. He found that when you Collaborate with your team, then you liberate Creativity and breed a sense of Commitment as never before. He had used that model when working with Ford Motor Company and reports that it contributed in part, to their getting the Taurus car in production faster than previous models thus saving tons of money. Not bad.

Managing Impressions

I enjoy the faces of the people in my audiences when asked, "What is a multi-billion dollar business in California that is based upon the identity of a rodent?" They go into a contemplative, searching and somewhat competitive space. I give them another hint; "the rodent has a best friend who's a duck" Got it? Disneyland, of course. How did anyone build an empire based upon the identity of a mouse? It was simple, though not necessarily easy. It seems, from what we've read and then experienced, that Mr. Disney knew that he was in the business of managing impressions and intentionally creating feelings in the hearts of his guests. If you've been to Disneyland, for example, you know that you walk into a pristine setting, filled with smiling employees, streets so clean that you could 'eat off of them', and an environment that is totally and intentionally structured to make you feel great. I can recall being at a "T" in the road there where the kiddyland is to the left and the frontier area is to the right. How do you know? Well, the left has wafting odors of cotton candy and sounds of the goofy cartoon music and the right has odors of barbeque and sounds of a plucking banjo. Somehow, I don't think these things were there by random accident. It's like one huge performance stage. They even call their employees "cast members". Everyone on staff knows that they are in the business of creating impressions. Create and manage your environment to create and manage the impressions of your guests. Simple, not that easy. It begins with the awareness, which thanks to Mr. Disney, we now have.

Idea:

Discuss this concept with your staff. Ask them if they can give any other examples of what Disney does for their guests. Examples might include Nordstrom's pianos, GNC's multiple item discounts, Wal-Mart's greeters and row of mega discount items, etc.

Ask them what impressions and feelings that they want your customers to feel and think about them. Then discuss what they could do to intentionally manage your customer's feelings and beliefs about them, you and your business.

Un 'Matched' Service

I will never forget an experience that I had at a restaurant just outside Denver, Colorado.

Knowing that it was a pretty fancy place, I selected it to impress an individual that I was interviewing to run a territory for a publishing business I established some 3 years prior. My business expansion was based upon our ability to find and keep quality managers to run out distant locations. When I made the reservations, I recalled that they were emphatic that I gave them the correct spelling of my name, a procedure that they apparently do with all reservations. The reason why was answered when we were taken our table. The host seated us, lit the candle on the table and

David Corbin

presented the matches to me. The matches were imprinted with my name on it. It was totally impressive. That created an atmosphere of professionalism that really captured the attention of that guy who became our regional manager to our mutual benefit... and made me so aware of the importance of taking the extra effort to create impressions... if not legends. The food and service were excellent as are many of my dining experiences. As good as they were, they were certainly not discussed as often as the "matchbook" experience.

Creating Negative Impressions

After a long shift on the casino floor, some of the employees would sit out front, slouching, smoking, drinking coffee and generally decompressing. Then, they would get in their cars, head home and come back for their next shift. While it is certainly reasonable that they do this, there is one challenge. Where they did this was right by the front entrance to the casino. This wasn't one of those large Nevada venues, it was a startup Indian casino housed in reconditioned trailers, not uncommon in these startups.

The challenge is that their presence was creating an impression. Remember, it is either creating a positive or negative impression, and is never neutral. So, which was it? Did the entering guest say to her spouse, "Look honey, look at those hard working employees regrouping after serving their patrons so that they could go home, wash up and return to serve us another day." I doubt it. They probably said, "Look at that. They have so many extra employees that they can just sit around and do nothing. Well, they're not going to take away my hard earned money to pay those bums."

Until these clients of ours were financially set up to bring in a trailer as an employee lounge, and armed with this new awareness, they set up a picnic table in the back for the employees to do their thing. The employees were appreciative of the effort made on their behalf and the entire team was then engaged in opening their eyes as to how they were being seen by their guests.

Idea:

Take your staff thru the exercise of exchanging their eyes for those of their customers. First, have them discuss just how they want the organization to be perceived. What impressions do they want to instill? How do they want their guests, customers, patients, clients, you name it, to feel about them, think about them, know about them, say about them, etc. With that established, have them go on a scavenger hunt to discover things that are either leading TO or FROM those desired impressions. Regroup with those ideas, put them up on the board and discuss which ones are feasible to change. We've done that exercise many times and it really engages the staff, fosters a sense of ownership, fosters a Psyched on Service awareness and is the one of the best and least expensive ways of making and keeping customers ever.

Creating Positive Impressions by Habit:

Great example of changing impressions. A young man was employed in the capacity of bingo card checker at one of our client companies. This young man was tall, thin and apparently well groomed. His hair, however, was long, down his back, and placed in a ponytail. The elderly Palm Springs bingo patrons were, from what I had heard, sometimes overheard talking about his hair and how he didn't know if he was a boy or a girl. Not atypical for those who grew up and missed that long hair era themselves. With that background, here's the story. This young man saw an elderly woman approaching the stairs that made the bingo hall a tiered venue. She was walking with the aid of a wheeled walker. As the story was told to me by some of these gray haired bingo regulars, the boy saw the lady approaching the stairs. He ran over from his position some 20 feet away to help. The story goes on to say that while they couldn't hear the conversation, the boy said something to the old lady, she smiled up in his direction, and he kindly assisted her up the stairs with her walker. Now, this is not exactly the effort that would qualify for sainthood. It was, though, a very nice thing to do… especially in a tiered arena where many people could notice.

I left those ladies who described that event to me and went over to the other side of the arena to link up with the General Manager. Then, as he and I were greeting one another, I overheard one lady (remember that this is way across the room from where those ladies told me the story) saying to another lady, "did you see what that nice boy just did?" That small but lovely effort had apparently caught the attention of quite a few people. We speculated that with that nice accommodation to the lady that some observers changed opinions from, "look at that boy, he doesn't know if he's a boy or a girl with that ponytail." to "did you see what that nice boy just did!"

Idea:

Discuss this story with your group. Ask them if they have any similar stories of small efforts creating big appreciation. Then, discuss ways in which they can create their own situations that are worthy of "legend s" and passing on to others.

By transforming the culture of your workplace, by making the company's success everybody's individual goal, you'll have shown them way to deserving their success. You'll have contributed to their control over their own destinies. And that control is critical not only to the individual professional's self-worth, but to the importance, they place in the company's success. Their mission jives with your mission. Is that the definition of co-mission? They'll be involved. They'll be happy. They'll be more productive than you may have thought possible. You work for it and The Psyched On Service Mentality will work for you!

Chapter 8
Clients Discuss Applications of Psyched Concepts

This is a transcript from a mock conversation among Business Leaders who have implemented the Psyched On Service (POS) systems.

Mortgage Banking CEO (CEO)
Interior Design Center Sales Manager (Sales)
Medical Equipment Manufacturer Marketing Manager (MktMgr)
Optical Retailer Director of Training (Train)

(Sales)   We started the POS with a meeting that discussed the concept of job security as the book describes. We did a discussion on the two requirements for anyone to feel job security and had each person focus on their core job functions. They liked the exercise and it not only gave greater clarity on their key job areas but also gave them the security of knowing exactly what our expectations are of them. The net result over time has been an increase in productivity and confidence. Moreover, it didn't cost anything!

Our start was similar except that we asked our managers to try to guess what their employees' top motivators were. Then, we compared their findings to the findings of the other managers and supervisors as mentioned in the book. After that we discussed what the employees said were their top motivators. We reviewed those motivators and discussed the top 5 things that we could do differently to meet the needs of our people.

(CEO)

Did you start making changes right away?

(Train)

No, we made a list of the top motivators, and then we rated ourselves on how well we were doing each of them and decided to focus on the rewards and recognition area. We asked two managers to head up this project and report to the group with suggestions on how we could keep the morale and motivation up by meeting their needs to be appreciated. That was the start of the program 2 years ago and it is in effect today.

(CEO)

Our company already had a reward program in place. What we did not have was a way to

(MktMgr)

keep our people "Green and Growing" as the book recommends. So we reviewed the section on motivation and did something similar to what the C.E.O. did. In addition to having the managers guess what the employees said, we had our employees fill out the questionnaire. Then we asked the each employee, from new hire to manager, to rate our company on how well we were meeting those needs and recommendations on what we could do to improve. This was done with an anonymous form. We got over 78% of them back and learned a lot of great information and some fantastic ideas that we began working upon.

(Sales)

When we bought the book, we were looking for ways to make our customers even more delighted with our services. Our focus was on creating legends. We did an exercise that asked our group of salespeople and customer service representatives the following questions, "what are some negative legends about our company and industry?" and "what are some positive ones?" That really got the ball rolling. Then with that, we discussed how we could increase the number of positive legends that were being told about us. Each job function met as a group and proposed five areas of customer "moments of truth" that could potentially create a legend. Then, as a group, they kept their eye out for the opportunity to create a positive legend. That same week, our telephone support representative department had created its first legend. We celebrated it like you could not imagine. Balloons, streamers, cake and some real loud high fives were prevalent. Now every department is looking for ways to create exceptional service... and finding them.

Has anyone used this system in the hiring process?
(Train)

We did. It was really pretty simple actually. We asked the people questions that would reveal their attitudes toward work and the workplace- ones that would reveal whether they had the right fit, as referred to in the section on 'skills vs. attitudes'. Our goal was to make certain that the new hire would fit into our culture and our mission statement. With that, we felt that if they qualified well or even marginally, that we could more easily build upon their skills than their attitudes. It seems to be working well. Our turnover is radically reduced while our productivity is growing.
(CEO)

Has anyone used the Units of Conviction?
(CEO)

We have. In fact, we are the ones that are referred to in the book. We have our volunteers using the Units of Conviction as they interface with our patients at the medical centers. It gives the volunteers greater
(MktMgr)

confidence and sends a consistent message to our patients.

(Train)

We use them too in our internal marketing signage. Our guests have some wait time before a concert begins so our staff developed a series of four Units of Conviction and we project them on the screen before the concerts begin. We interspersed them between slides advertising upcoming events. It adds to our credibility and strengthens our relationship with our guests.

(Train)

One thing that we adopted quickly from the book was a formalized training on service recovery. Our staff was not consistent on their methods. Sometimes they came across defensive, angry and upset... when they really were not feeling that way. So we did a workshop on the six Step Method, made our modifications to the process to custom fit it to our environment, and began to use that method. We put up posters in the offices and places that our employees would easily see. Our people adopted the methods fast. We think it is because it was co-developed by them, not just shoved down their throats. Then, in meetings, we would discuss specific situations where we tried the recovery process and how it worked for us. We celebrated people doing it well... and we celebrated people doing it fairly well. They tried, they went for it and we showed them the respect due. I suggest that every company adopts this part because it helps the customer, helps reputations, gives employees' confidence and everyone wins.

I would suggest strongly that the communication skills module be applied to all front line employees. I mean including the receptionist, the customer service people, the maintenance people and every employee that has any contact with the customer. I say that because we had no idea how poorly our front line communication was. We had no reason to inspect that interaction for effectiveness because they were not the primary interface with customers. Our focus was more on the salespeople; the direct customer support people and those job functions. However, we came to realize that there were other job functions that were creating major impressions on our customers... and we had not proactively set up any training to positively control or influence those interactions. We had the supervisors of these areas read Psyched. We asked them to put together a 2-hour workshop (and offered assistance as needed) on communication skills. It was a relatively new skill for them but they loved the challenge. It was fantastic the way that they collaborated with the other supervisors and developed the workshop- like a team building

(MktMgr)

exercise. Then they rolled it out with their people and it was great. Now we made it a part of our new hire orientation and the supervisors take turns leading that part of the process. We are big champions of teaching and reinforcing positive communication skills.

(CEO)

We did an interesting exercise that worked well for us. Remember in the book where David was talking about the Reticular Activator System? He talked about opening up our mental filters to certain things. Well, we took our staff and discussed the concept of looking at our medical clinics through the eyes of our Patients. We first discussed how we WANTED to be perceived. Then we discussed David's point that we are either moving forward or backward toward making an impression; that we are never neutral. Our group was then given an opportunity to go on a scavenger hunt looking for examples of things that were either moving us toward the way we wanted to be perceived or away from it. After the 30-minute scavenger hunt, we reconvened and discussed the lists. It was amazing. It was such an eye opening experience. We saw things that were virtually invisible before. We then made a list of things that we felt could be fixed or changed for little or no investment of time or money. We also made a wish list for other things that needed to be changed that did, indeed, require funds. We agreed to do this every quarter. Now we have everyone serving as a visual quality control monitor, making sure that we are sending out the right impression, creating the desired environment and, essentially, wearing the eyes and ears of our Patients. It really makes a difference.

In Gratitude:

Many thanks to the following people for having so influenced my work and my life: Mark Swerland, Bill Campbell, Dale Halaway, David Pemberton, Victor Risling, Brian Tracy a true Master Teacher and Mentor, Mitch Axelrod, Dr. Dan Delgado, Bill Diller, J. R. Greene, Peter Robben, Bobbie Rubin, Gail Kingsbury, Steve Lyman, David Gilman, Mitch Rutledge, Dr. Larry Macapagal, Dr. Ralph Steinberg, Eric Werts, Michael Patrella, Mary Lou Stephan and the deeply committed Kaiser Permanente PVS Team of Doctors and Staff, Mike Byelick, Danny Garrett, the one and only GoalsGuy Gary Ryan Blair, Harry Paul, Pat Zigarmi, Mark Victor Hansen, John Meech, Joel Weldon, Bob Wylie, Sheldon Moss, Dr. Don Gold, Reymundo Reyes Martinez, Alvaro Urago (mi hijos), Jack R. Mitchell, Albert Atallah, Carolyn Seligson Mickelson, Al Pappas, Robin Blank, Rabbi Wayne and Ellen Dosick, Chmn. Mark Macarro and the Pechanga Band of Luiseno Indians, Chmn. Anthony Pico of Viejas, Ron Richard, Jim Cathcart, Bill Gerber, Denis Waitley, Mike Romagnolo, Chmn. Dean Mike of 29 Palms Band of Mission Indians, Michael Gerber, David Mickelson, Hon. Sec. Jesse Brown, Max Yazgar for allowing some half million friends & I to camp out his land 1969, Ellen Domb, Poway Blackmountain

Toastmasters, Roz Natal, Aunts Sydell Cohan and Flora Shorr, Uncles Bill Cohan and Sanford Shorr, Lynn Campbell, Rick Sims, Noah Rolland and the great management team at Rancho La Puerta, The Pechanga Development Corporation Board, Anthony Miranda, Butch and Patrick Murphy, Bob Moyer, Haig Kalegian, Mae Hartley, David Leibowitz, Bill Salinas, Dr. Steve Schneider, Ron the Con Millette, David Smith, Kevin Thornton, Bob Romano, Barb Schwarz, Kirk Bohrer, Joe Stumpf, Phil Del Prince, Carole Osborne Sheets, Cathy Bucalo, Mark Weinberger and Mary Millosovich.

John Carroll, the wordsmith extraordinaire, has been the most valuable contributor to the crafting of this book.

For your insight, input, direct and indirect contributions I say, Thanks all.

My Dad, who is up there giving them a run for it in Heaven, taught me more than can be written here. He was one tough cookie. He was a proud prizefighter, war hero, politician, union leader, husband of over 50 years, father, and grandfather. His example of tenacity, respect for and utilization of common sense (he said we all have plenty of it because not many use it much anyway), and general 'can do' attitude have inspired me my entire life. Mom you are still my role model for unconditional love and caring. I cannot thank you enough for the sacrifices you made to help with college and everything we ever needed, then and now. Thanks Mom and Thanks Dad.

My business life support system is embodied in one person, my administrative assistant, Jeannie Aguire, who is the most wonderful colleague in the world. Thanks Jeannie.

Index